On Impact

ONIMPACT
LIFE, LEADERSHIP AND BETTING ON YOURSELF

BENNY POUGH

NEW YORK

LONDON • NASHVILLE • MELBOURNE • VANCOUVER

On Impact

Life, Leadership and Betting on Yourself

Published in New York, New York, by Morgan James Publishing. Morgan James is a trademark of Morgan James, LLC. www.MorganJamesPublishing.com

Proudly distributed by Ingram Publisher Services.

Morgan James BOGO™

A **FREE** ebook edition is available for you or a friend with the purchase of this print book.

_____

CLEARLY SIGN YOUR NAME ABOVE

Instructions to claim your free ebook edition:
1. Visit MorganJamesBOGO.com
2. Sign your name CLEARLY in the space above
3. Complete the form and submit a photo of this entire page
4. You or your friend can download the ebook to your preferred device

ISBN 9781631958403 paperback
ISBN 9781631958410 ebook
Library of Congress Control Number:
2021951287

Design by:
Christopher Kirk
www.GFSstudio.com

Contributor:
Jaylaan A. Pough

Morgan James is a proud partner of Habitat for Humanity Peninsula and Greater Williamsburg. Partners in building since 2006.

Get involved today! Visit MorganJamesPublishing.com/giving-back

*For my mother, whose love, support, and friendship
exists beyond the confines of space and time.
Her spirit is forever with me.*

TABLE OF CONTENTS

ACKNOWLEDGMENTS

First and foremost, I would like to thank God, for His favor, mercy, and consistency in my life. To the surgeon who saved my life in the accident, Dr. Terrance Curran, thank you for using your magic hands to repair my broken body. Thank you to my wife and children for supporting me through my wins and shortcomings. To Benjamin Pough Jr., thank you for your fundamental recipes on becoming the best man I can be. And finally, thank you to the On Impact team: Dedra Tate, Rian-Ashlei McDonald, Renita Bryant, Michelle Ghee and Raoul Davis, as well as my editing team at Rain Drop Creative.

PREFACE

"**A**s iron sharpens iron, so one person sharpens another," has always been the foundation of my relationship with Benny Pough. Seventy-two hours after Benny strutted into the Def Jam Records office for the first time, I had no doubt he was a mover and a shaker.

On that day, I had assembled an independent radio team to distribute Kanye West's, *Thru the Wire*. Mind you, this was pre-fame Kanye, but don't get it twisted—the infamous ego was in full effect. Benny led the overall radio promotions when the *powers that be* weren't sold on *College Drop Out*, or for that matter, Kanye the

Rapper. Because I vouched for Kanye and *College Drop Out*, it was my responsibility to get traction on his inaugural song. So, I rolled my dice with Benny, who, at the time, was the Head of Radio Promotions at Def Jam. My trust was not misplaced: Benny made *Thru the Wire* a mainstream hit. The song launched Kanye's career and was the impetus to my multi-decade brotherhood with Benny.

To put it mildly, Benny is a magnet. Early on, I was drawn to his deep-rooted integrity, charisma, and commitment to his word. He always does what he says he's going to do. Additionally, Benny is contagious in the way he interacts with people and always makes sure that everyone around him feels comfortable and valued. These values have become the cornerstone of his identity. Whether you are the CEO of the label, a superstar artist, or the intern bringing him a bagel, he will never "big time" you. When Benny enters a room, it lights up: what he brings to the table can't be taught or bought. Day in and day out, from the first time I shook Benny's hand, he has shown himself to be a true leader. After the acclaim of *Thru the Wire*, Benny and I worked on the next three singles Kanye released from *The College Dropout* album.

Parallel to the Kanye promotions, I had another song, *Can't Stop Won't Stop*, that I needed to push. Our process was akin to a two-part assembly line at a factory: I brought the record, and Benny did his magic. He strategically placed the records at certain stations, he knew when to release the songs, and he consistently implemented a custom-fit, comprehensive strategy for each single.

Early on, Benny was instrumental in securing some of the biggest hits we achieved at Roc-A-Fella Records. One of our shared experiences that resonated the most was our successful work on *No Better Love* by Young Gunz and Rell. At that time, I witnessed firsthand Benny's passion, stamina, and high spirit. We spent an entire day in his office as he played the song at least thirty times. He would scream over and over at the top of his lungs as if I were two blocks away, "Yo Biggs, you sure?" He kept looking at me and hollering across the desk, "You sure this is it?" We listened to that song on "repeat" until we knew every verse and every note.

After a drink or two, we signed off on it and then went to work promoting the single. The song shot up to the Top 10 and broke 5,000 spins on the radio. It was an early win which confirmed to me that Benny was not only a star, he also knew how to make a four-teen-hour workday feel like a lively hour-long lunch.

In writing this foreword, I had to abandon my professional relationship and my personal friendship with him and ask, "Why is Benny the right person to write this book?" I did not have to think about it for long because the answer was simple: few people make it out of neighborhoods like those Benny and I were born in, and those who do make it out, do not always prioritize giving back like Benny does. In addition to this, *On Impact* is a road map for young Black men to keep pushing forward despite life's challenges, while supporting their communities along the way.

I earnestly believe that this book will be inspirational to indigenous communities all over the world. It will be a blueprint for the average person who doubts himself and does not know how to succeed beyond his surroundings. Early on in life, I could have benefitted from the lessons found in this book. I experienced my own apprehension and doubt and often found myself on the fence. I believe that Benny's straightforward, transparent, no-nonsense story of persistence and hard work will have a snowball effect which will, undoubtedly, impact many lives for years to come.

Benny also has succeeded through true grit over the long-haul with rarely matched production skills and exceptional performance in the music industry. Benny is a pacesetter. His team can barely keep up with him. Benny embodies work ethic; the one trait I look for in a co-worker, along with honesty. His integrity, commingled with his stamina, is what separates him from others and is the fundamental reason that he and I see eye-to-eye. I can call him at any time of night, and he will be there because Benny never stops. That is the kind of person you want in the trenches with you when you are trying to build any kind of company.

The other attribute that stands out when I think of Benny is his vulnerability. When he trusts you, he turns off his edit button and lays out so much that you, in turn, feel comfortable telling him your innermost thoughts. In fact, when Benny and I get together, it is a lot of, "Man, I never told anybody this," or "I never told anybody that." When Benny shares his stories with me, there is always that "aha!" moment. I have gone through many of the same things he has gone through, and it is rare that Benny and I disagree on anything. The few times we have had an opposing thought, one of us says something that makes sense and draws the other over to the same line of thinking. The "bridge" that truly brings us together, more than anything else, is that we are two men of faith. Our bond is rooted firmly in our relationship with God Who is always at the center of our lives.

I profoundly look forward to many decades of grinding, building, and winning with Benny, as well as helping as many people as humanly possible along the way.

—Kareem "Biggs" Burke

INTRODUCTION

Everything fell into place the summer before my fortieth birthday. During this time, my son tested for his black belt in Taekwondo. This was a big deal since he had trained from the age of four and had been fast-tracked to get his belt before he turned seven. Leading up to the final exhibition, the kids had to complete a few tests to prove something to the trainers (or maybe it was all about proving something to themselves). Each test was different. Though my son was prepared, this was his first competition, and it would be the biggest challenge of his young life.

One afternoon, he came into the kitchen and told his mom and me about another test for his black belt: he had to take an egg to school the next day and look after it without breaking it. Outwardly, I showed no concern and just nodded my head as a show of understanding. However, when I glanced over at my wife sitting at the kitchen table, I raised my eyebrows and gave the universal, *"Are-you-hearing-what-I'm-hearing?"* look. She laughed. She was not worried because he had already done well in the previous tests, and she thought we should have more faith in him. I get why she believed that, but since I am being real, I figured that there was no way he would make it back home with his egg still intact. My wife ended up being right. The next day, my son walked through the door with his egg in one piece and a broad grin on his face.

During another challenge, members of the team had to stay overnight in the mountains for three days with no electricity. They were required to remove all distractions and, instead of being consumed by the outside world, they bonded, trained, and prepared. While that task sounds less complicated than looking after an egg for an entire day, imagine taking a group of always-connected kids and adults and planting them in an environment where televisions, cell phones, and social media are nowhere to be found.

My son was learning a lot through the tests and seeing him achieve each one taught me a few things, as well.

* * * *

On the morning of the exhibition, I knew that my son was prepared, but something was not right. As a parent, you know when your kid is acting strange, and they seem a bit… off. However, because my son is typically even-tempered, his stoic expression could be confused with focus or concentration. As a parent, I knew it was more than that. The competition was a big moment that carried enormous amounts of pressure. The kind of pressure that turns coal into diamonds or bursts pipes.

Yes, he was prepared, but now he had to rise to the occasion. That was the first time I thought about what was happening. Being fast-tracked sounded good and created a few bragging rights, but now it was about execution and the weight which rested on his young shoulders.

By the time I found my seat on the sidelines at his exhibition, I was concerned and wondered if he was truly focused on the gravity of the moment. I asked my wife if he seemed okay, but she thought I was overreacting.

A few minutes before he was supposed to test, I asked my wife again. This time, we both saw a difference in his body language. His posture was not straight, and he looked unfocused. I caught his attention and motioned for him to meet me in the bathroom so that we could talk. I asked him, "Son, what's happening? You are not focused. What's the problem?" Even though he was fully prepared, he explained that he was feeling a little nervous and unsure. I told him, "This is your moment, and you have to see the finish line to cross it. You can do this! You have worked hard for this for three years, and this test is only a few minutes. A few minutes does not equal three years of hard work. The math just does not add up. Understand?" He agreed and walked back into the gym with newfound confidence. "I know you can do this!" I said again, hoping my words were getting through. I whispered a quick prayer and retook my seat. I could tell him repeatedly that he could do it, but doing it was solely his part. I just hoped my words would reassure him. A few minutes later, I had my answer. I watched proudly as he took his position, broke multiple boards, and earned his black belt in Taekwondo.

Here is the thing: I knew that I had to say something to instill enough confidence so that my son could master that moment and all the future moments he would struggle to overcome (especially as a young

Black man). That is much of what life is: a bunch of moments we must master, or at least maneuver, with unshakable confidence in who we are and what we can accomplish.

It is not about having fears, because we all have fears. The goal is not letting our fears deter or defeat us. It is not allowing fear to hold us back or keep us from becoming something greater or from achieving something bigger. We lose too much time when we allow fear to hold us hostage, and by God's Grace, my son was not going to be another man whose fears would make him a prisoner of his own mind.

* * * *

Not long after that day, I came face-to-face with my own mental roadblock. To bring in my fortieth year, I wanted to do something monumental, so I decided to run my first marathon. Not just any marathon, though. I wanted to run the New York City Marathon: 26.2 miles through the five boroughs of the city. Although most people train for months, I chose to do the opposite. The longest run I had done prior to the day of the race was sixteen miles in New York City, from the West Side Highway to Brooklyn. Other runs during my training were from three to five miles. I do not know if it was a Superman complex or just foolish thinking, but I was going to run the marathon with no training and little experience.

On that chilly November morning, I woke up amped and ready to run. I put on several layers of clothing along with a pair of running shoes. When I looked in the mirror, I felt the impact of this milestone. Once I was at the assigned starting point, I looked around at the growing crowd, feeling more as if I belonged. It was everything I had imagined it would be when I made the decision to sign up.

From the starting point at the Verrazano Bridge through the first few miles, my body responded to the cheers and encouragement of volunteers and spectators. Our energy matched step for step. With every clap, I ran faster, breezing past my fellow runners like a fake Usain Bolt. I felt good and was certain I looked strong. I could already picture myself at the finish line.

Then something shifted. About fifteen miles in, I hit a wall — not a literal one, but a physical and mental one. Because I had not trained, I failed to realize that I had been running too fast from the start. Consequently, fatigue set in, and I had only reached the Queensboro Bridge. Fifteen miles in, and I still had a little more than eleven miles to go.

Although a few onlookers shouted words of encouragement, I felt as though for me, the race was over. "*There is no way I can finish,*" I thought to myself.

Not only was my mind defeated, my body was beyond its limits. Everything either felt numb or exuded pain. I considered my options, and I do mean *all* options. I did not want to be like Rosie Ruiz, the woman who cheated in the Boston Marathon back in the 1980s. Since I was connected to a GPS race-tracker app, I could not cut corners or leave the race without my family knowing. I looked down at the runner's token on top of my shoe and closed my eyes. I was tired, out of energy, and out of options. *"Real talk, I don't need to run a marathon. Why am I doing this? It is not like Nike is sponsoring me to run. Why did I even sign up for this race?"* I negotiated with myself as thoughts of bowing out and throwing in the towel filled my head.

Then I pictured my son. Earlier that morning when I had phoned home before the race started, he told me how proud he was of me. I thought back to his black belt exhibition and how I had pushed him. I remembered the look on his face when he received his belt—a symbol of his hard work and achievement. What kind of man would I be if I cheated or failed to finish? How would I help him through life's toughest moments if I could not master my own without being dishonest? It was not about one race or one day. It was more than that. Not finishing would always hang over my head, and I would never forgive myself for giving up. Moments like this can make or break you as a man.

I had to be able to look my son in the eyes and at myself in the mirror. There was not another option.

Serious runners will tell you that training for a marathon means increasing your distance little by little until you find yourself running up to twenty miles before the official race day. However, I did not train like most people. Prior to the marathon, I had only dabbled in running. On my own, I had run less than ten times, the longest distance being sixteen miles. *Sixteen* was my magic number. Every step beyond that would be a milestone in and of itself, and would require more from me, physically and mentally, than I had ever given. But there was still that wall I had inevitably hit and, with it, the urgent need to either stop or sit.

Suddenly, as I came off the Queensboro Bridge and onto First Avenue, I caught a cramp in my right leg. At that point, stopping became a legitimate possibility. I reached for my leg as it bent backwards, too afraid to put my full weight on it again. I winced as I slowed to a snail's pace, now focused only on limping to the fluid and massage station a few yards ahead. With every step, the sharp sting radiating through my leg became less bearable, and my once strong and consistent stride had become a faint hobble.

I staggered over to the station and rushed toward an available chair. My body collapsed onto the small contraption, and within a few seconds, a pair of hands worked to loosen the cramp in my leg. I savored every second of that massage because it brought me a few minutes of peace before rejoining the other runners on the course.

While I was coming over the 138th Street Bridge in the Bronx and then down Fifth Avenue in Harlem, it happened again. Five miles had passed since my last massage, but my body knew it was time for another one. I could feel myself slowing down and cramping up. When I returned to the course, I came up with a new game plan. I made the massage stations my new markers and indicators for progress. If I could get from one massage station to the next, I would eventually finish the race.

Without proper marathon training, I was ill-prepared and had no concept of what it meant to run 26.2 miles. It's amazing what the body can do once the mind is set. When I decided that quitting was not an option, I was unstoppable. One step at a time, I propelled myself toward the finish line. It was grueling, painful, and not something I ever want or need to do again, but I did it. I finished the New York City Marathon.

Thoughts have the power to either force us forward or pin us back, scripting the narrative to our victory or our defeat. But allowing fear to win will make you a failure one hundred percent of the time. When you focus on being the best, accomplishing your best, and operating at your best, you may not win the race, but you're guaranteed to finish it. Wanting to maintain my son's respect, and my own, superseded the pain pulsating through my body. Of course, being mediocre is always an easy option, but I want to be great. And great is more than a higher level... it's a whole new dimension.

This book is another dream. From cover to cover, it's filled with stories about a lifetime of lessons and decades of moving step by step to reach goals often considered insurmountable and unattainable. At times, situations fell into place like words of a well-written song. Other times, they unraveled without warning. I have experienced the highs and favor of success, and the lows and solitude of mistakes. Both have taught me, without overtaking me.

Ultimately, *On Impact* is the blueprint to how I got where I am today. Every good and bad decision is packaged into these bound pages. However, let's be clear... nothing about my story is neat. It wasn't neat to get divorced, quit jobs, or almost lose my life; yet in still, these glitches are all part of my story.

The path to success is rarely straight and unencumbered. Rather, it consists of curves and roadblocks that force you to rely on personal conviction, consistency, creativity, and a bunch of common sense. Very often, it was in doing things that left me out of the limelight from which I reaped the greatest rewards. These gave me a foundation because by the time I became president of anything, I'd already been operating on a presidential level (or at least proven that I could). It didn't happen overnight.

I love everything about music, and in about every job I have had in the industry, the music loved me back. I started during a time when music was evolving, but the mindset of industry leaders didn't always match up. The gap between the two gave me room to solve problems and make an impact. Over time, I learned the difference between being on the inside where you create and make decisions about how music is packaged and sold, versus the outside, where you consume it and decide if what you have is what you want. I've spent years rooted in both worlds. Even now, I am an architect within the industry and someone who appreciates and encourages the art the industry produces.

In late 2018, I was honored with the inaugural Urban One Honors Record Executive of the Year Award. Being acknowledged was the culmination of years of grinding and laying groundwork throughout my career as a music industry executive. It acknowledged my work in an industry (where minorities are not always at the head of the table), making the important decisions. I appreciate the Urban One team for recognizing my years of commitment and dedication.

All individuals must face their own black belt exhibition: the achievement of a goal for which they prepared, but still feel unworthy when it's time to execute the task. Or, they may have to face a marathon: an overwhelming challenge for which they haven't prepared and are on the verge of throwing in the towel. The difference between those individuals who reach the finish line and everyone else is IMPACT: Intuition, Mastery, Pivot, Authenticity, Connection, and Teamwork.

It's one thing to want to reach a high-ranking title or celebrity status, and another to do the work and invest the resources to earn it. IMPACT means setting intentions even when others offer shortcuts. It is demonstrating mastery and drive on days when you don't feel like getting out of bed. It is prioritizing your time because the option to quit cannot be a real option. *On Impact* is about having a vision for what you want in life and following through, even when the road ahead is unclear.

We've all been in the position where we think we have it figured out one minute, only to find ourselves scratching our heads in confusion the next. As a business leader, I have learned just as much about myself through the setbacks, as I have through the successes. In other words, being open to the lessons learned within life's disappointments is just as important for my growth and success as my achievements and accolades.

From my first job at the age of eleven, growing and evolving have been integral and inherent parts of the process. The burning desire within, the part of me that knows who I was born to be, and the special talents I possessed when I entered this world, will not allow me to give up or give in. That part of me has never accepted complacency.

Over the years, I have met great people, led amazing teams, and had front-row seats for the launch of more than a few best-selling artists. *On Impact* is a glimpse into my travels on the road which I took to get to where the architect intersects with the art. Each page brings more insight, and it is hoped that by the end, you'll have more answers than questions. This opus is not merely about what you want. It is about creating a legacy of which you are proud.

HEADING NOWHERE FAST

Something told me not to go. It was Labor Day weekend, and I was exhausted from trying to keep up with my own demanding schedule. My childhood friend had invited my family to his barbecue, and I was running an hour behind schedule. Between the severe weather, traffic, and distance, we would not get there for at least another two hours. In view of these challenges, picking up my wife and daughter and getting to his house in time felt impossible.

Earlier that week, I was in the middle of a business call and briefly clicked over to let my friend know that I would call him back. He said that he wanted to invite me over for a barbecue, and without thinking, I told him that we would be there. I didn't think much about the commitment for the next few days, but had I checked my schedule, my response would have been somewhere between a soft "*maybe*" and a hard "*no.*"

On August 30, the day before the barbecue, I flew to Charlotte, North Carolina, then drove ninety minutes to Columbia, South Carolina, to attend my nephew's football game and spend some quality time with my sister and her family. We then went to Orangeburg, South Carolina, to celebrate our father's seventieth birthday with more family and friends.

As I anxiously waited in the airport for my return flight back to New York on August 31, a voice came over the intercom to let us know that the flight would be delayed. A few hours later, I was grabbing my luggage and rushing into the city for a midday meeting. The delayed morning flight, mixed with my going downtown in the middle of the day, threw off my schedule and pushed everything back. I still had to get home to pick up my family before heading to my friend's house.

Any of those reasons was enough to back out, but I had given him my word, so I kept it moving.

I have known him for more than eighty percent of my life, and know that he is all about the details. Everything he says has action behind it because he is a planner and doer. Two days after I accepted the invitation, he checked in to confirm that we were still coming. The next day, he called again to re-confirm. Finally, he called the day before the barbecue to check in and confirm *again*. I had given him a firm "yes" on each call.

By the time I arrived home to New Jersey, a sudden storm had settled into a light, misty rain. I considered driving the convertible but changed my mind once I realized that my daughter would be in the back of it and in a vulnerable position. We decided to take the truck instead.

Even though we arrived two hours late, my friend and his family were welcoming and forgiving. I wasn't surprised to see all the food and serving dishes spread out. However, I *was* surprised to learn that my wife, daughter, and I were the only invited guests. Now his multiple confirmation calls made more sense.

Turns out that the entire barbecue consisted of four adults, two children, and at least three bottles of wine. We were surprised, flattered, and glad that we didn't cancel. Throughout the afternoon, we talked about everything from family and work to vacations and our health. Later in the evening, my friend and I moved to the rear deck to continue discussing what was happening in our lives: things that were going well and things that were too painful to mention. As we talked, the light rain began again, and a heaviness filled the air between us. Trying to shift the mood toward something less serious, one of us suggested that we take a ride in his new Benz. We thought it would be a good diversion and inject a bit of lightheartedness, as well.

Things appeared normal as I followed my friend from the rear deck of the house through the kitchen and out to the carport. After a few comments about the design and features of his new car, he went into the house to grab a cigar before stepping back out and hopping into the driver's seat. Then, I jumped into the car and he and I buckled our seatbelts. As he turned the music on, our families came outside. We smiled and waved to them as he backed out of the garage, turned the car around, and drove forward out of the driveway, which was the distance of a New York City block.

As he approached the end of the driveway, he opened the gate, and we made a right turn onto the street. Outside my window were sprawling lawns, only slightly concealed by gated entrances. The opposite side of the street consisted of a wooded area filled with trees and untapped potential. As we moved along the two-lane road, I took out my cell phone, intending to make a quick call. A forward thrust just barely knocked the phone out of my hand. Out of nowhere, we accelerated. I looked out of the corner of my eye to see the speedometer moving past seventy miles per hour and headed towards ninety miles per hour in what had to be a thirty-mile-per-hour zone.

"*What the heck!*" I yelled, confused. Don't get me wrong, I have done my fair share of showboating in a new car, but we were grown men with families. We had more to lose now, and I was not interested in masking recklessness as excitement. When I turned to look at him, he was unconscious and slumped over with his foot planted on the accelerator.

Panicked, I tried to get my bearings. I shook him and yelled, but he was out cold. As I sat up in my seat, looking back and forth from him to the road, I realized that the end was near.

For the everyday person, there is no way to prepare when something like this happens. There isn't a course that trains you for the moment you come face to face with your own mortality. Most of life is spent doing the opposite; figuring out how to outlive and outlast. It's about fighting every obstacle and using it as a stepping-stone toward whatever achievement or goal is in front of you. However, my current obstacle wasn't some trivial thing that barely registered on life's scale of importance. It was the devastating reality of my impending death. It was witnessing my own transition from one life to the next. I wanted to yell and scream and use every ounce of energy within me to get myself back into the house with my wife and daughter. I needed to be in the office, working, or back in South Carolina with my parents and sister. I wanted to be anywhere but, in a luxury, car speeding down a residential street with a passed-out driver, and yet, all foreseeable conclusions pointed towards me winding up dead.

My chest rose as the air circulating in my lungs became more suffocating than freeing. I knew I needed to breathe, and I wanted to, but as the car's acceleration increased, so did the truth of what was happening. I squeezed the door handle with my right hand and prepared to brace myself.

A stillness overcame me. I thought, *"What am I supposed to do?"* Instinctively, I knew. My mother had already planted seeds for moments such as this. She raised me to call on the only protector I knew, especially when everything seemed bleak. Without hesitation, I spoke to God. I thanked Him for His blessings in what now seemed like my last moments: *"Lord, I guess I'm not going to see my family again. I guess I'm about to see you soon. Who's going to take care of my family? What about my mother? She has Alzheimer's. Who's going to walk my daughters down the aisle?"* My thoughts were a mix of prayer and confusion.

The day before, I was fortunate to celebrate my father's seventieth birthday with my family. A week prior, I had dropped off my son at boarding school. Now, I was heading toward the end of my life. There would be no more birthdays or celebrations. A lump formed in my throat as the weight of what was happening came into full view: *my family is about to bury me.*

We sped past house after house, going faster with each second as everything became a blur. I gripped my head and considered my options. There was no time to act and even less time to think. Anger arose from within me as I thought, *"Am I going out like this? God, is this really it? I always figured I'd die doing something heroic, but this? Is this how it really ends for me?"*

Veering off the road, we clipped several bushes and trees. Every time we hit something, his foot would bounce up off the accelerator, giving us a moment of reprieve before it hit the pedal again. Suddenly, we struck an object in the road, redirecting our path. The Benz swerved from the right lane across the left and jumped the curb. Once again, I braced myself as the last image I had was the front end of the car barreling across broken limbs and heading toward a massive oak tree.

* * * *

Excruciating pain radiated throughout my body. Disoriented, I blinked several times, hoping to get my bearings and grasping the gravity of what had occurred. I reached for the door handle, but quickly realized it was stuck. I later learned it was jammed because it had warped during the crash and had become cemented to the oak tree. Loud screams and moans filled the car as I tried to get out. I felt an unyielding soreness emanating from my abdomen. The unending sounds filled my ears before I realized that I was the one screaming. My friend was still unconscious. I don't know how the first responders removed the car door, but suddenly, a cool rush of fresh air surrounded me.

"Don't move! Sir! Don't move!" I heard a muffled voice less than five feet away. I continued to yell as the policemen and paramedics worked to free me from the car. "Sir, what is your name?" asked a voice nearby. "Benny," I said in a rushed whisper, hoping that he would bypass the questions and focus on making the pain stop. Instead, he continued to test my memory as I went in and out of consciousness.

"Sir, what day is it?" he continued. My head hung forward, slightly limp, yet settled in its anchored heaviness. I writhed in agony, praying one adjustment, even if marginal, would provide a modicum of comfort. Fearful shouts of, "Is he okay?" and "Benny!" filled the space between us. "*Hold up, is that my wife?*" I thought.

She was standing in the distance, being held back by police officers and emergency workers as I was barely conscious and praying no part of my body was lodged underneath the dashboard of the car. I blinked several times attempting to tone down the severity of the bright lights. I wanted to respond, to reassure her that I was okay, but I couldn't lie. Instead, I asked the guy to hand her my watch and keys. It's interesting what you think about and prioritize in certain moments.

I became more erratic as the pain increased from unimaginable to unbearable and my probable death became my focus. I couldn't imagine that a human being was built to endure such physical hurt. I was convinced that this had to be a precursor to death.

As I was cautiously removed from the car and onto a nearby stretcher, an officer grabbed my hand. As he began to speak, his positive energy was palpable and, in an instant, I understood the depth of that human connection. "You're gonna be alright. You're gonna be alright," he repeated calmly as I winced and writhed. His eyes bore into me as if he could bring me back to health. After another few seconds, he released my hand, and someone else spoke.

"Sir, we have to get you to the hospital. You have two choices. We can transport you in a helicopter, but it'll take twenty minutes for it to get here and the ride will be bumpy because of the storm. Or, would you prefer the ambulance, which can leave right now but may take longer to get there?" He bent down as he asked the questions, trying to make sure I understood my options. Honestly, all I wondered was why he was asking me. I was in massive amounts of pain and while I didn't know exactly what was happening in my body, I knew death was quickly approaching. The last thing I wanted to do was take a pop quiz on two modes of transportation leaving a location at different times, while also trying to figure out which would arrive at the destination first, with me still alive. *Forget the calculus.* Admittedly, I was angry for being asked the question and for having to decide.

"Agghh! I don't know! Help me!" I grunted, through cries of agony. The first officer grabbed my hand again as the second officer repeated his question about the ambulance versus the helicopter. I yelled for the ambulance because twenty minutes sounded like the equivalent of an eternity. Once the words left my mouth, the second officer yelled instructions, and someone else came over to help wheel me away from the car and onto the ambulance. As the officer continued to hold my hand and tell me everything was going to be alright, the pain coursing through my body intensified. The emergency workers opened the ambulance door and counted off to lift me from the ground to the bed of the truck. The officer released my hand, and the energy I'd been grasping onto dissipated.

Behind me, I heard someone ask him, "How does he look?" As I struggled to remain conscious and remember his words of comfort, the last thing I heard before the ambulance doors closed was his reply. "I don't think he's gonna make it."

LESSON 1:

INTUITION

T he first letter in the word "IMPACT" is "I" for "Intuition." Intuition tells us, instinctively, what something is without our having to analyze it. I know you've walked into a room, and immediately felt whether the vibe was dull or fun. Have you ever immediately met someone, and you just knew you'd be good friends? How about sensing danger? That's intuition. We all have it. It's up to us whether we act on what intuition is telling us. Following this chapter, you'll find my "Intu-

ition Hit List": a few takeaways that I hope you'll think about and incorporate into your life.

CREATE AN OPPORTUNITY OR AN ADVANTAGE

Work has never been a foreign concept to me. From an early age, I witnessed the inextricable relationship between work, money, and freedom, and understood the benefits of controlling all three. Over the course of my life, I have held fifty-eight different jobs; knowing that number should give a clear indication of how proud I am of that fact. It also shows how dedicated I am to having control over my own destiny.

My first job was born from a selfish motivation. Every summer, my parents would send my sister and me from New York to Orangeburg, South Carolina, to spend time with our relatives down South. Even though we knew it was coming as the school year's end approached, the urgency with which our parents packed us up and sent us away was always surprising. Regardless of which day the school term ended, my parents had us in the car and on the road by Friday of the same week, without delay. If school ended on a Friday, we were on the road headed South later that same day. My parents, looking to pick up extra hours at work, paid my grandparents to keep us during the summer. In fact, many of the grandkids came down. I would say we had our own summer camp, except we worked more than we played.

My grandparents lived on a farm, which meant that, over the course of approximately ten weeks, they had a litany of tasks that needed to be done and a bunch of children with enough time on their hands to do them. We did everything from feeding chickens, hogs, and horses to picking peas, peanuts, pears, and watermelons. For them, it was free labor. Labor mattered during those times and in that environment because the land supplied everything else. Most farms produced for two objectives, and my grandparents' objectives were no different: to sell and to consume. We ate what was in season and sold everything else. Looking back, the setup was fair, worked well, and allowed everyone to contribute to the family (even the kids). But, at the time, my mind was set on my own freedom, not objectives and fairness.

One summer, my uncle took a few of my cousins and me with him to load watermelons in the back of his pickup truck. I stepped onto the truck's bed, prepared to do my part, and fulfill my role in the multi-person assembly line of catching and stacking melons. Although the process varied, depending on how many people were involved, it typically went the same way. The first person picked up the melon from the ground and tossed it to the next person who was a few steps closer to the truck.

That person tossed the melon to me, and I stacked them in the truck bed until it was filled to capacity.

After a half-hour, I was sweating, tired, and physically drained from the blistering heat. This country life was not my thing. Once we were done, we drove over to the intersection of Russell and Windsor Streets in downtown Orangeburg to sell the watermelons for a quarter each. Although it was honest work, and plenty of people support their families in similar ways, it wasn't for me. As I stood there, a young Black man on the corner selling watermelons for a quarter, I realized there was little compensation for all the grueling work we had put in. I wanted my summers to be different. At that moment, I was determined never to do anything where the value of my labor was not reflected in the pay or end reward.

I was a metropolitan kid, and I had to produce a way to avoid those long drives and sweltering summers. Unfortunately, complaining did little to sway my parents. I needed another way out... something they could not refuse. *I needed a job*. First, it was a credible reason for not going back to work at the farm. Second, a job would put money in my pocket, which I soon learned was its own form of freedom.

Even Children Get Hustled

By age eleven, I had already started delivering papers for *The Reporter Dispatch* in White Plains, New York.

Being up before the sun meant my mornings started just as some people were settling in from the night before. My commitment was to have the newspaper in my customers' yards before they opened their front doors and before I started school. There was little value for a morning paper in the middle of the afternoon, so hitting snooze and sleeping in were never options. Mornings consisted of slow movements and several blinks before I could function. Before long, my young mind and body became accustomed to waking early. However, a few cups of coffee would have made those mornings much easier.

The following year, when it was time to pack up and prepare for another summer in the South, I devised a plan. I went to my father and gave him the facts. There was no way I would be able to keep my paper route if I left for two months. Did he want me to lose the opportunity? Also, I was making money delivering papers, but it cost them money to send me to South Carolina. Without realizing it, I was learning the art of negotiation and persuasion. With little hesitation, he agreed, and that was the end of my summer trips to the South.

Having a job taught me many lessons. Some were expected, while others were surprising and less appealing. Of course, there are the obvious things like critical thinking, problem solving, money management, customer service, responsibility, and commitment. Decades passed before I called that experience what it was: entrepreneurship. I was an entrepreneur long before it was a trending topic or a hashtag. Dedicated to making sure my product was where it needed to be when it needed to be there, I managed inventory, oversaw weekly transactions, and handled customer complaints.

The process was straightforward. The local paper manufacturer would advance me a certain number of copies of the daily newspaper. I would distribute the papers and then on a specified day, go to each customer's home to collect payment. Every Saturday, also known as "collect day," was the day I had to pay the paper its share. The dispatcher would drive to various locations, and all the kids would bring him the paper's share of their sales.

There were four basic rules. First, you had to have the money. Second, you had to go directly to the location to avoid being robbed, since it was a cash business. Third, you always counted the money in front of the dispatcher and took your receipt as proof. It was never wise to hand him an envelope with the money inside without counting it in front of him because he could take some for himself and then say you were short. Finally, the dispatcher did not care if you were short—only about the balance due. You had to keep the sob stories to yourself.

By far, the biggest lesson I learned through paper delivery was unexpected. As a young businessman, I learned that adults have no qualms about hustling a child. Not every adult is honest and being a child does not alter that truth. Some adults have a low threshold of integrity. Many customers tried to pay me half the balance due, with promises to pay the remainder in a few days or the following week, only to lead with another excuse once that date came. Some would find ways to justify not paying at all.

Do you know how difficult it is to get people to pay you after they've already received the service or product? If it's their intention not to honor their commitment, it's almost impossible! I had to figure out ways to manage shifty adults who paid late or did not want to pay at all. My boss at the *Dispatch* expected a payment on collection day, regardless of my customers' excuses or lack of funds. If I wanted to be profitable, I had to minimize the chance that my percentage would be used to repay the paper's split.

I was dedicated to the job and never allowed weather conditions, sleep, or my age to be a barrier to following through. I believed that if I did my job and met my end of our agreement, my customers would hold up their end. Unfortunately, that wasn't true, and some people only wanted what was best for them. They received exceptional service, but some chose not to tip or to even pay at all. The paper route taught me a lifetime of lessons that never left as I grew older.

Seeing how the moving pieces worked in business lit a fire in me. From that moment on, I would always get what I was owed, and in a timely manner. No one would be able to deny what was due to me. What I earned was mine, and insignificant excuses would not deter me from reaching my goal.

Cashin' Out With Friends

Three years later, I was hired at a well-known fast-food restaurant. During my first two years, I was promoted from fries to burgers and quickly became a crew chief by the age of fifteen. Legally, I was only supposed to work up to twenty hours a week. However, one week I worked sixty hours. If hours were being processed legally, I would have received triple overtime pay (or never worked that many hours in the first place)! Instead, I was asked not to mention it and was paid time and a half to keep the company's books clean. Decades later, as I reflect on the overtime hours filled with cleaning bathrooms, replacing hot grease, and flipping burgers, I realize how much the company exploited its employees.

Working alongside me at the restaurant were many of my friends; a dynamic that created its own share of lessons. Being crew chief meant I had to impose the rules and often press others to do their jobs. It also gave me the ability to identify problems (or opportunities) and come up with solutions.

One problem I noticed with many of my friends was what I liked to call a *paycheck predicament*. Because most of them didn't have bank accounts, they weren't able to cash their paychecks without involving their parents or losing a sizable portion to a legal (or illegal) check-cashing business. While working and having their own income was a huge step, a barrier still existed for them to fully enjoy it.

Since the age of five, I've had a bank account. I can still remember proudly walking into the bank with my mother to deposit my savings in a Christmas Club account. Witnessing the paycheck predicament while having my own bank account meant I could offer a profitable solution to my friends and coworkers. The plan was simple. On pay day, we would travel to my bank where I would have my friends endorse their paychecks over to me. I would distribute everyone's pay, minus a small percentage, which I kept as a processing fee. Those early years managing the paper route taught me the importance of paying myself first. Everyone benefited from our operation, and it showed me how to create win-win solutions.

Hustle Harder

During my junior year of high school, I started cutting class to go to gambling parties. Now, most of the guys attending were street savvy and more seasoned at hustling than I was. While I played fair, they played to win. Naiveté put me at a massive disadvantage, which would become obvious much later.

One day, my mother handed me $1,200 and told me to pay the annual insurance bill by that upcoming Friday. She and my father were headed South to visit family and needed me to handle the bill while they were gone. Because they would be out of town for a few days, my house was the obvious choice for that week's gambling party.

My "friends" arrived with $5,000 to $10,000 each, and Blackjack was our game of choice. As we played hand after hand, I found myself losing increasingly. After losing my original $500, I went upstairs to retrieve another $500 from my room. I returned to the table only to find myself $1,000 lighter in a matter of minutes. I kept expecting my luck to change with every hand dealt, but I was sinking rapidly with no clue as to why. They were hustling me, and I was oblivious because I was focused on game rules when, only street rules applied.

Once I felt the sting of losing every penny I had, I ran back upstairs and grabbed the insurance money. I would like to say I hesitated for a minute, that my better judgment or some semblance of a moral compass kicked in and urged me to reevaluate my decision.

Honestly, only for a second did I consider the possibility of losing it. I was confident I could climb out of the hole and turn around my losing streak. My ego would not allow me to walk away knowing a chance at winning was not only possible, but probable. I knew what needed to be done. With confidence, I went back to the table and gambled every dollar until it was all gone.

They beat me out of $2,200. On Monday, my parents were due back, and I still needed to pay the insurance bill. You know what creates ingenuity? Urgency, plus a few drops of desperation. Immediately, I thought about ways to make extra cash. I went through my room and chose clothes and electronics to sell. I borrowed money from friends and associates with promises to repay plus interest. Because I had a car and many of the other kids in the neighborhood did not, I started charging people for rides. Seriously, I was the original Uber. From chauffeuring friends and driving people to work to delivering food from the deli across town, I hustled until I earned back the money. I walked into the insurance company and paid the bill without ever having to utter a word to my parents.

Opportunities are Often Created

Early in my career, I brimmed with an overwhelming desire to be successful and make an IMPACT. I always sought opportunities that would get me closer to my goals instead of relying on others to chart the path for me. Not everyone saw the potential in a situation, especially when it was not glamorous or if it required them to go against the norm. By the time I hit my twenties, I was a father, and had to rely on a balance of humility and strength. A big ego or small thinking would have stifled my progress and limited my options.

My first internship was with Motown Records. Everyone there consumed canned beverages. Over time, I noticed how many cans were being thrown away. Before long, I saw an opportunity. I knew cans could be redeemed for five cents each, so I brought in a cardboard box and put it near the intern area. I asked people to rinse out their cans and place them in the box. I was likable and well-regarded within the office, so soon, everyone obliged and started throwing their cans in the box instead of in the trash. Once the box was full, I would take it to the recycling center for payment.

Not worrying about how others would perceive me or the fact that I was making money from selling cans helped me put gas in my car, kept food on the table, and enabled me to clothe my daughter. I was only making fifty dollars per week at Motown, which was not enough to cover child support, transportation, or other expenses. Despite this, I refused to allow my ego to get in my way. Every moment, opportunity, and dollar counted! The key was to focus on the greater goal and never allow my ego to overshadow it. It was another win-win for everyone involved. It began as a creative business opportunity for me, and it became an effective recycling initiative for Motown.

INTUITION HIT LIST

- ❏ You will not be prepared for every opportunity, but every opportunity will be presented to you.
- ❏ Opportunities are often buried within moments of complacency.
- ❏ Situations that appear simple may be the perfect setup for future success.
- ❏ Do not lose focus or settle just because an environment is familiar.
- ❏ It is your responsibility to make the most of what is going on around you so that you can get closer to achieving your goals.
- ❏ Don't worry about doing the same thing as everyone else. It is all about infusing INTUITION into everyday opportunities.

LESSON 2:

MASTERY

The "M" in IMPACT represents "Mastery." Mastering your craft is obviously important, but you must also master yourself. "Mastery of self" means knowing who you are, what you want, and how you are going to get the things you want out of life. When you have mastery over yourself, you are not stuck in your comfort zone. Instead, you are willing to take chances when they are presented, to reach your personal and professional goals.

DON'T SETTLE FOR GOOD ENOUGH

During my college years, I secured summer jobs with General Motors. First, I worked on the assembly line, and then in security. At that time, summer jobs were nothing more than a means to make money; they weren't about long-term gain or future opportunities. My goal was simple. I wanted to earn as much as I could in a short period so that I could enjoy financial independence when classes started back in the fall.

When I applied and was subsequently hired, I was excited because having General Motors under my belt boosted my resume. Moreover, making twelve dollars an hour with overtime potential meant big paychecks at the end of the week. To repeat, my objective was to make as much money as possible. There appeared to be no downside until I went in for the job.

During that summer, I was a screw gun operator. I installed the same six screws into the same holes in the front and rear armrests of every Pontiac (6000 were manufactured during that time), with no thought or critical thinking required. Over and over, and over again, I heard the annoying sounds of drilling, screw after screw: *buzz buzz*—pause—*buzz buzz buzz*.

For an entire summer, that was the soundtrack to my life. It was agonizing and to make matters worse, I had to stand the entire time (eight to ten hours a day), while walking up and down the assembly line. Due to tedium, some people complain about work and don't understand their privilege. More so often, they work in places where they can get up to use the bathroom with no hesitation or grab a cup of water without needing permission. On the assembly line at General Motors, I learned a different definition of *work*. Every minute of every hour was spent producing, and if we wanted to use the bathroom, make a call, or do anything that most people take for granted, we had to first be relieved from our post. Do you know what it feels like to work every single minute of an hour? Really think about it. Every. Single. Minute.

I went back to General Motors the two following summers but chose, instead, to work in security. Although I realized my time at General Motors wasn't my dream job, it taught me what I was made of and that, even in less-than-ideal circumstances, I could and would still achieve. I had identified goals (making money to afford certain freedoms and building my resume), and I was determined to do whatever was necessary to accomplish them. That experience also further established my strong work ethic, commitment, and ability to perform and produce in undesirable circumstances.

People committed many egregious acts throughout my time at General Motor: everything from gambling to theft. Although those are serious acts, nothing came close to triggering dismissal like walking off the line or leaving a post without being relieved.

The summer after my sophomore year of college, I returned to General Motors. I had already decided that although the money was great (there were weeks where I earned $1,500 with overtime), the work was not something I wanted to do for the rest of my life. I no longer wanted to be driven by money. Sometimes, we stay in temporary jobs for a lifetime because we hold on to them long after their expiration date. That was not the life I wanted, so I concluded that my summer job would not hold me hostage beyond that summer.

On the last scheduled day of my employment, I left my post without being relieved. It was the only way to ensure I would never be able to go back as General Motors would not rehire someone who had broken its cardinal rule. It was one thing to mentally decide not to fall into what was convenient. It was another thing, however, to take away the possibility altogether. That day, I cut up my security net. It was the only way to push myself past familiarity and convenience so that I could achieve my goals.

When I reflect on that day, I am convinced that walking away was the most irrevocable way to show my commitment to my dreams. There was a calling within me that pushed me to excel, but I had to make a big investment in myself. I first had to believe that it was possible by letting go of Plan B and giving myself time to grow and evolve without settling into other people's expectations. Walking away further demonstrated my devotion to a potential future that had yet to reveal itself. It was the ultimate show of faith in God and in myself.

I reiterated this point recently while talking to my children. It was important for them to know that every move I've made in my career was meant to push me closer to achieving my own view of success. I did not build a life and career based on luck and chance. I operated strategically and deliberately. How would life have been different had I not defined my goals and bet on myself? What decisions would I have made if instead of thinking, strategizing, and planning, I'd chosen to purposelessly wander, hoping I was on my destined path? What if I had followed other people's plans for my life, or even tried to mirror theirs? What if I had gotten caught up in the impressive titles or celebrity interactions and become complacent because what I had was already good enough? When you have it really good, it can derail any chance of achieving *greatness*.

As a teen, I could have focused solely on the amount of money I made at General Motors but being led only by money would have altered my entire life's path. Instead, I envisioned what I wanted and got clarity on what was needed to achieve it. I removed what was convenient and familiar and replaced it with investing in my future. At the same time, several questions remained in the back of my mind: *"How can I get from where I am to where I want to be? What exists in my life to help me get closer? What should I remove from my life that has the potential to hold me back?"*

As I elevated in my career, the choices, and sacrifices that I made to achieve IMPACT meant different things. Sometimes they meant working weekends. Other times, they meant taking business calls around the clock, even while on vacation. These minor impositions may not have been acceptable to some, but that was okay with me because I knew how those choices would impact my getting to my *why*. I learned early on that having a goal and knowing what you want makes decision making much easier. That certainty includes how you spend your money, energy, and most importantly, time. Early on, I wanted my children to think about their lives and the choices they needed to make so that decisions would become easier in the future. I never wanted them to know the burden of indecision because it could significantly delay or even disrupt their path.

Stumbling Forward

Some of the best and worst moments of my life happened during my time at St. John's University in

Jamaica, New York. While my days were spent learning theories and concepts, I split my evenings between family and a rotation of four different jobs: performing standup comedy at local comedy clubs, driving limousines, working as a security guard, and selling cutlery door to door.

At the age of twenty-one, I married my high school sweetheart. For a brief period, we were happy, living, and working toward what I believed was our shared dream. Not long after reciting our vows, we had our daughter. Neither of us had the experience to understand what marital commitment truly meant. We struggled financially, had no plan to change our condition, and thought love would cure it all. Against the better judgment of her parents, we jumped into the marriage feet first.

Although it is important at any age to be cognizant of what marriage and commitment signify, it was especially true for me at this point in my life. We had little idea of either concept when we recited our wedding vows. At the time, we believed that we were ready and understood what we were stepping into. Our minds were fixed, and there was little to be done about challenging or changing them. We thought her parents were wrong about us not being ready for marriage, and our plan was to show them the error in their thinking. Nevertheless, hindsight brings clarity, and life soon showed us that we had no idea what we were doing.

Eventually, our marriage fell apart. Upon reflection, I can see how my definition of love has shifted over the decades. I learned that sometimes the feelings and expectations accompanying such a complex situation change, and not always in the way we predict or plan. For example, all the control I believed I had was merely imagined.

I think it was the stress of so many bills, along with our being simply too young to handle marriage. Neither one of us had been married before. I mean, there's no handbook for this kind of stuff. We had no idea that our marriage could be so challenging. We'd set out to show her parents that they were wrong when, in fact, we were just proving them right.

On our best day we didn't have effective communication skills. On our worst day? Well, let's just say we didn't shy away from yelling at each other. The sad thing was that yelling didn't make things better. We both saw it going in the wrong direction and had absolutely no understanding of how to get it back on track.

It became increasingly difficult to focus on my studies while things were in such disarray at home. The stress of trying to maintain the façade that everything was fine to those around me was simply too much to bear. Something had to give, and unfortunately, that something was my schooling.

Coming home every day and having arguments about everything other than the real problem was just so draining. Neither of us could get past the anger at seeing one another or the resentment which lingered between us. While I knew my grades were slipping, I wasn't able to do much about it. I was simply ill-equipped to handle so much stress at one time. I was young and immature in my way of thinking, and that is easy to recognize now.

A failed marriage was never part of the plan for my life. We were supposed to be married forever, and I was supposed to graduate with my degree and become immensely successful. I would take care of my wife and my family, making a living doing something I loved. Yet in still, it was not to be. As much as we cared and loved each other, we were floundering, unable to fix what was wrong. My life was off the rails and nowhere near where I imagined it to be.

All the stress from home really had an impact on my schoolwork. I was a wreck. I couldn't concentrate, my mind always filling with an endless cycle of "what if" thoughts. I stopped attending classes and fell into a lull. The following semester, I received four F's. Something had to change. Potential failure was palpable, and life was getting out of control. Even at my lowest point, I knew that I couldn't stay in that mindset for too long. It wasn't like me to sit and sulk or admit defeat. I had no choice but to rebound.

There was no way I could succumb to the weight of my predicament because my parents had saved and invested to put me through college. Quitting was not only about me, but my entire family, as I would be the first to obtain a college degree. I couldn't have my parents think their sacrifice was in vain.

Recognizing the gravity of my situation, I humbly met with my academic advisor. I told him the truth and asked the obvious question: "*What can I do to get out of this predicament?*" Although his face was stern, his eyes were empathetic as I relayed the details of the past few months. After I finished talking and answering his questions, he said that I would be placed on academic probation and could stay at St. John's if I received four A's at the end of the next grading period. I was thrilled to have another chance to prove my value, but wondered, "*Could I get four A's?*" I was expected to become a straight-A student in a matter of months. It wouldn't be easy, but at least I was still in the game. I had a chance to redeem myself and get back on track. Years later, I understood the significance of talking to my advisor in person and not leaving it to email or even a phone conversation. This was a critical turning point in my life and required face-to-face interaction. Being able to sit across from one another and put a face, voice, and expression to the situation created authenticity and connection. I told my story before assuring him of my commitment to do better as a representative of the University, my family, and myself. That day, I mastered how to tell my story and position my "ask" in a way that helps the other person to be able to help me more easily.

The following semester, I received three A's and a B+. That's good, given the starting point, but *getting close* to four A's was not our agreement. I went back to the head of my department, knowing I had to sell myself once again. I pitched him on why I needed a second chance to prove myself. Even though I missed the mark, he recognized my effort and allowed me another chance.

Despite my pulling things together enough to graduate and earn my college degree, things kept getting worse at home. It was exhausting, my being so angry and miserable all the time. I finally had to pull the plug. Just before my twenty-fourth birthday, we divorced. Now we faced an even bigger challenge: how to effectively co-parent our daughter.

While the decision to divorce was a difficult one, we had to make the hard choice. We needed to separate for both of us to thrive as individuals. Staying together would have only prolonged the inevitable, and we would have lost valuable time. Once we decided to go our separate ways, we were committed to what was best for our daughter and for one another.

Even though I understood what was happening, the life change occurred so fast that I hadn't braced myself for the impact. I went from being the head of household in a small family to being a divorced father. If there ever was a *rock bottom for* me, I landed there in my early twenties.

During this time in my life, I was ill-prepared to handle the emotional blows I suffered. I stumbled and lost my footing, and it took time to pull myself out of the mess I'd made… but I did it. I dedicated myself to learning, growing, and doing better the next time around. I used the stumbles as input to my own maturation, and I sped ahead with a different urgency. Time is our most valuable resource, and the last thing I wanted to do was waste it.

Setbacks teach us many lessons. Losing love, family, and my own false narrative of what I was supposed to do and be, shaped my life in a powerful way. It's okay not to be a superstar or have life all figured out. People should step back and take time to figure things out, including how to master the path meant for their life and not that of others. Hitting rock bottom turned my life around in ways I had never imagined. I became more focused, driven, and understood the value of making tough decisions. Years later, I remarried and began my corporate career in music. I never forgot my time at St. John's and used it to fuel my growth. In the end, what was meant to break me helped to strengthen and to build me up.

Can You Handle the Truth?

The pitch to my academic advisor showed me the importance of narrating the story of one's personal brand. Whenever I walk into a new organization, establishing my brand and ethics within the company is paramount. Regardless of which title or position I hold, my personal ethics matters: I value them and am intentional about maintaining their quality. What I represent, who I am, and how people perceive me will either help or hurt any conversation or business deal. No one wants to invite you to the table if you have questionable morals.

"Hi, I'm Benny Pough." is my standard introduction. I always include my first and last name, and never just say Benny. Leading with my personal identity humanizes the interaction and reminds me of my principles and convictions. My name sources back to my parents, my upbringing, my hurdles, and my successes. It is the embodiment of a lifetime in two words, and those two words center me. They won't allow me to be an empty suit or a false representation of everything for which

I have worked. Regardless of the company employing me, my principles guide every interaction. As a result, having a keen sense of self has led to better relationships, partnerships, and opportunities, both personally and professionally. It has also kept me out of situations that could have distracted or derailed me.

As a leader, owning and managing your equity is the cornerstone of wearing your brand. What do people think about you when you are not around? What do they think of you based on what you have made them feel? What adjectives do they use to describe you? What words would you want people to use to describe you to others?

You can manage your equity only if you are aware of it, and awareness starts with asking questions and being willing to accept the answers. It also means implementing the feedback. What good is having people give you valuable information and if you are not willing to utilize it? Leadership and humility go hand in hand. Although it is sometimes uncomfortable to be reminded of our imperfections, it is necessary if we want to achieve proficiency. Great leaders learn early to master self-awareness and reputation management. I want people to associate my brand with high-quality work ethic and superior results.

As a music industry executive, I was not allowed to underperform Not merely because of my title, but because of my convictions. I am constantly learning to stay current in the industry. Being a consummate student gives me the ability to innovate and progress beyond today's market trends. Likewise, the work ethic I developed through my paper route as a child is the same work ethic I have today. It is what keeps me hungry for challenges and resolved to find innovative solutions. However, as stated earlier, I cannot perform at my highest level if I am unable or unwilling to accept the feedback from my team, peers, management, and loved ones.

Mastering your equity also means managing your external image. Some may not admit it, but how you present yourself does impact how people perceive you (even in business). Your choice in something as simple as what you wear to a business meeting or event can shift people's perceptions of you and your career. Craft your style, with the intentions of your career goals in mind, and own it fully.

Stay Ready So You Don't Have to Get Ready

I've been privileged to sit down with a variety of people from all levels of society. This extends from sitting presidents to OG's. Since the topics, languages, and locations of every interaction are different, my clothing selection changes accordingly. I must be flexible, and that means having a diverse wardrobe that can flex along with me. There's no need for last-minute shop-ping or worrying about anything that pops up on my calendar. Leadership entails being ready to do the work as well as being *perceived* as someone who *can* and *should* lead others as they do the work. Attire allows us to express ourselves and reveals our personality long before a single word is spoken. Great leaders master how they represent themselves to others.

I coach members of my team on reserving some aspects of their personal style for home versus the office. They learn how to adapt to the system, at the beginning, and earn room for greater self-expression after proving themselves. I've found that company leaders give latitude to people they value and want to keep around. By increasing your productivity, you earn the right to color outside the lines a bit—unless, of course, you were hired to disrupt. Then, you play by an entirely separate set of rules.

* * * *

Like that of most people, my life has been filled with incredible highs and undeniable lows. Every situation has offered me a chance to learn more about myself and to choose how I want to show up every day. There was no other way to overcome shortcomings in my early twenties than to move forward with dignity and respect. Trying times may bend us, but it is our choice to refuse to be broken. Know that everyone has a superpower that can be used to his or her advantage. Establishing and amplifying your "superpower" is the first step to mastery. Authenticity will open doors and create bridges to the right people, the right conversations, and the right situations.

Rising through the ranks of the music industry and landing in positions of authority could have changed me, could have made me either a magnified version of myself or a representation of what I believed I was supposed to be. Having a keen sense of self combats the urge to become a man I can't recognize in the mirror. My IMPACT relies on the sacred commitment never to become comfortable looking at myself and finding a stranger staring back.

Always Bet on Yourself

When I was interim Head of Urban Promotions at MCA Records, I came to know a senior member of Artist & Repertoire (A&R) who had signed notable acts like New Edition, Bobby Brown, and other superstars of the era. He asked me to pay attention to one of his artists, considered a rising star. I had not heard of Jesse Powell, but after asking around, I understood that label management had already marked his project as unimportant and not worth additional investment in time nor money. Therefore, the company wanted to terminate the A&R person and drop the artist in one strategic move.

After servicing the record to radio nationally, only three markets took a chance on Jesse's single *You*. In St. Louis, Missouri; Little Rock, Arkansas; and Norfolk, Virginia, it was the number-one played song in each market. Those successes demonstrated potential, and although management continued to disagree, I stood my ground and joined the A&R executive in reading the tea leaves. I knew that it would be a hit if given the chance in additional markets. The only issue was that it was an uncertain time for me at MCA. I was new to the position and was the last man standing after a regime change. Now, my actions showed that I was defiant to what the establishment wanted, but I knew what could happen if my instincts about Jesse's record were right. While in the car heading to the BET Awards that year with the general manager of MCA, he told me, "If you choose to promote this record and it doesn't hit... you're fired!"

There are always defining moments in your life or career, and this not too subtle threat was one of mine. I had worked so hard for many years to have it come down to one song and one moment. From delivering newspapers to becoming a vice president at a major label, it all came down to a single decision. It was the culmination of everything for which I had worked and sacrificed.

I could have acquiesced and aligned with management to end the record, drop the artist from the label, and not support the A&R executive. It would have surely been an easier path forward. I was getting married in a few weeks and had a planned honeymoon a couple of weeks after. My manager knew all of this, yet he still chose to share his sentiment in the back of the limo on our way to an awards show. At once, I fully comprehended the widely used phrase, "business is business." Since my management cares about results and the bottom line, I asked myself, *Do I shoot my shot or pass the ball? What if it doesn't work out and I lose everything I have built? Is it worth the sacrifice?* A multitude of questions replayed in my mind as I considered all sides.

I chose to step out on faith and aim for success. While the days of my honeymoon were spent making calls promoting Jesse's record on radio, evenings consisted of celebrating with my very understanding and selfless wife. There was no other option except rising to the occasion and doing what needed to be done. Multiple careers were on the line, not just mine. I followed my instincts; the result was exponential, and the record became #1 on the R&B charts. I had a pulse on music, promotions, and success from Jesse Powell's *You*, and demonstrated it to the industry.

Opportunities show up throughout our lives, and often when you least expect them. Situations and timing are rarely perfect, leaving some unprepared to take on the challenge and others ready to rise to the occasion. If there's a chance that taking your shot will result in achieving your goal, never hesitate to take it. When you believe in yourself, trust your instincts and are confident in your value, all things are possible.

MASTERY HIT LIST

❏ Your smartest decision may include cutting up your own safety net.

❏ Acknowledging your faults and struggles will help you build towards your goals.

❏ Don't be afraid to break away from your comfort zone to get to where you are supposed to be.

❏ Stay ready so that you don't have to get ready.

❏ MASTER your craft so that you have the confidence to take a chance.

❏ Bet on yourself!

LESSON 3:

PIVOT

I n our acronym IMPACT, the letter "P" represents "Pivot." Too many people become stuck in jobs, or even careers, in which they are not happy because they fail to recognize when it is time to make a change. For whatever reason, they don't pivot to see the next opportunity awaiting them, so it passes them by. Pivoting can be done over time, or in a split second. The important thing is to learn when to pivot, and that realization is what this chapter is all about. Learn to pivot for success.

SET YOURSELF UP TO WIN

As a child, I was one of those creative types. I tap danced and I tried various instruments in pursuit of what best suited my personality. When I was seventeen, I aspired to be an actor. I was so committed to the idea that I had a professional bio and headshot.

Although I was driven, I miscalculated the difficulty of breaking into the acting profession. Going to audition after audition without being cast made me question my decision to pursue my passion of acting. Then, during a casting call in Brooklyn, I got into a rousing conversation with another guy auditioning as an extra. He turned to me and casually said, "You're really funny! You should think about doing comedy." At first, I paid little attention to him, but a few days later, I gave it serious thought. Shortly after, I started writing comical material.

During that time, a new age of comedy was introduced. Harlem staples like The Uptown Comedy Club launched, and within a few years, television shows like *Def Comedy Jam* were attracting massive crowds. Young, aspiring comics had a place to grow and to launch their careers. Such opportunities had been less prevalent before. Prior to that time, an urban comedian could not penetrate the network of the largely white-only downtown clubs unless they were well-connected.

Although acting was my original plan, comedy held more opportunity and spoke to my natural instincts. Two to three nights a week, I performed stand-up comedy in New York, Connecticut, and New Jersey. Comedy was a different animal. Through the art and science of stand-up, I became more self-aware. It taught me who and what I was, and how to channel that into something bigger than I. Stand-up brought me face to face with my fears and vulnerability. I was able to work through them in my performances. Doing stand-up showed me that I was a salesperson at heart and by craft.

When on stage as a comedian, you put it all out there. People will either cheer, boo, or look indifferent. To be clear, indifference is worse than disgust. Imagine setting up your best joke and delivering a punchline, only to be met with silence and a blank stare. Choosing to be a stand-up comedian means choosing to have tough skin and to be completely vulnerable. You understand that you cannot control the outcome, only the inputs.

Stand-up was hard at first, but after I got used to the grind, I loved it. Soon, I learned to perform with confidence because none of the boos or indifferent stares were personal. Business was business. Those reactions happened to be some of the downsides to the business, but there were high moments as well. For example, when I absolutely killed a show and heard the laughter from the crowd and the thunder of their stomping feet, I did not need validation from others to keep me going. However, I valued the constructive criticism anyway.

While I enjoyed the world of stand-up comedy, there was a major issue. I was no longer providing only for myself. I had a two-year-old daughter at home with important needs like food, shelter, clothing, and healthcare. At twenty-five dollars per show, comedy took up too much of my time without enough benefits on the other end. I made the decision to find a job with higher pay and health benefits.

Although I walked away from a dream, it was the springboard to my start in the music industry. For years, I had tried not to be a corporate guy, but business was my thing. One night after a show at The Cellar Comedy Club, a woman recognized me and offered me an internship at Motown. I said, "Yes," and that was my entrance into the music industry.

Alone and Uncovered

The summer after my college graduation, I began my career in the music industry. Internship programs are prevalent and familiar today, but when I was asked to intern at Motown, I had no clue what the term entailed. I went from performing at a comedy club to working for the Northeast Regional Director of Promotions. It was a professional development program designed for a college student. However, since I'd already graduated, the director restructured the role and made it appear as a post-graduate opportunity.

Securing an internship at Motown was a big deal, but there was an important consideration. The program provided a twenty-five dollars per week stipend, which was meant to cover only basic travel needs for a student. However, I wasn't a student, and my needs extended beyond basic transportation. Although I knew the pay before I accepted the job, I figured the growth potential and contacts were worth the sacrifice in pay. I was focused on the long-term, but in the short-term, I was an adult with a growing child and responsibilities. My boss understood my situation and found a way to give me the regular twenty-five dollars per week through the internship program and an additional twenty-five dollars each week off the books. While the supplementary income was helpful, I still maintained two additional jobs by driving limousines and working security.

Motown is known for its indelible impact not only in the music industry, but society at large. With artists ranging from Stevie Wonder to Boyz II Men, I was thrilled for the opportunity to work at such an esteemed company. In high school, I was passionate about the idea of being an accountant, so my new role aligned with my interests. Each day consisted of processing travel expenses and filing reports.

While I was working one day, an independent consultant noticed how fast I typed. He was impressed and asked if I could also do some administrative tasks and bookkeeping for him. I later learned that few men in the business could type sixty words per minute, so I was a bit of an anomaly.

Over time, I started paying closer attention to the transactions that came across my desk. The company paid for my manager's travel, dining, fuel, phone, car insurance, and cable bill so that she could stay up to date on the latest updates and trends. On top of the perks, she received a paycheck. I thought to myself, "*There's a job for which someone will pay me to eat, drink, travel, watch television, and listen to the radio?*" Once it sank in that the answer was "*Yes,*" my new career goal was decided. I wanted *that* job.

* * * *

Within months of being at Motown, I transitioned into the role of College Promotions Representative and began to thrive. Selling was foremost in my new role, and fortunately, my background in comedy came in handy. I was considered personable and witty, which allowed people to lower their guard. A strong work ethic also helped, since I was always early for meetings, consistent, and dependable. Knowing that someone would answer on the other end of the line when you call was vital to my early success at Motown.

Unfortunately, all good things come to an end. After a couple of good years, issues with senior management persisted. The person who helped me move into my role was no longer working at the company. In addition, making a name for myself came with both good and bad consequences. Since my position was significant to the team, management executives wanted to put their own person in the role and allow them to ride the wave of my work. I was told that, while I would be able to progress and eventually be promoted, it would be at a slower pace than I originally thought. Fortunately, my former manager and advocate had taught me well, and I was able to navigate the situation.

Nonetheless, there are seasons in life and business, so my time at Motown quickly winded down. I could have stayed, but I had little reason to believe my staying was best. I tapped into my network and found an opportunity for a new position at a different company. The move allowed me to grow in the industry rather than stay and remain stagnant, having to prove myself all over again. If I had to do that, it may as well be with another company.

Growing at the Back of the Line

The president of a new startup label, Perspective Records, called as I was weighing my options at Motown. Even though the talent was not as well-known and the brand was not as recognized as my then-employer, I accepted Perspective's offer because the role expanded my range and elevated my title.

Moving from the front of the line to the back was eye-opening. People were slower to answer my calls (if they answered them at all). The opportunities were not as fruitful, and the company structure was vastly different. In contrast, Motown was the most recognized music label in the world. The name alone garnered respect worldwide. It came with a cachet and the assumption of greatness: a high-quality brand must inherently have great people. When I met someone as an employee of Motown, certain assumptions were already made, which meant I was able to have meaningful conversations earlier on. We could jump to the heart of a matter because my employer's brand was the foot in the door.

That all changed when I moved to Perspective. It was a new startup label. Therefore, I had to explain the company's mantra to any individuals I met so that they had an idea of what we were about and why it should matter to them. Clients weren't as apt to listen to unfamiliar artists from a new label without the artist's proven success. They also wanted upfront transparency on my need or "ask" of them, so they knew the objective of the interaction and could decide if it was worth their time. It took longer to get into the meaty discussions because of the layers leading up to them.

Motown proved to be a diligent school master. It taught me the value of integrity, dependability, and responsiveness. During the year I worked at Perspective, I learned how to build and expand my brand. Since we were new, people had to buy in to me. Nevertheless, I learned how to beat the competition without the resources of a larger machine behind me. It meant being nimble and more entrepreneurial. I did not change the strategy from my Motown days, but I did modify it. Ultimately, learning and evolving became second nature.

While at Perspective, I was the National Director of Lifestyle and Street Marketing, which is big business to this day. It is a promotional strategy of leveraging the "who's who" in a given market as your own grassroots street team, since they have their fingers on the pulse of what's happening within an area. Their job is to raise brand awareness, acceptance, and the purchase of your product. Consider them the originators of social media influencers long before any of the platforms were created. Eventually, the street promoters became label promoters, finding innovative ways to penetrate urban markets and untraditional ways of promoting new projects. They were connected to barber shops, hair salons, community centers, and gathering spots that our artists needed to reach.

In my career, being able to pivot has always been second nature, and I can feel when it is time to move on to the next opportunity. Perspective Records taught me two of the greatest lessons about having IMPACT:

1. Short-term thinking will get you pats on the back, but long-term thinking will secure your name on the wall.
2. Your relationships influence your influence.

In the music industry, there are very few African American corporate presidents. Even with three distribution companies and several notable labels, there are less than a handful of key African American figures involved in the decision-making at the top. That meant I had to set myself up for success for the long term, and not give anyone a reason to overlook or sideline me. I focused on the basics and laid a foundation for my own success, starting with industry knowledge, connections, and positioning. It all mattered: what I knew, who I knew and the rooms to which I was invited.

Later in my career, when I gained exposure to the full operations of a business, this acquired knowledge shifted my mindset and increased my understanding. It is imperative for me not only to be *in* the room but to be in the *right* room and involved in the *right* conversations. Also, being in the right meeting is more important than sitting in just any meeting. What is more, being in the right position sets you up to help get other people into those same rooms.

It took several years and a lot of great mentorship and guidance to learn that my greatest impact on an organization, in addition to contributing to the bottom line, would be having a positive influence and secure relationships with the people that I work with. After all, *IMPACT* means being in a position of true exposure and having widespread visibility.

PIVOT HIT LIST

❏ Where you are now is not where you will always be.

❏ The ability to learn new skills and expand your options rests in the everyday opportunities that come your way.

❏ If you are in the midst of a stagnant situation, change your direction.

❏ Never forget that your perspective is not the only perspective.

❏ Trust your instincts when you feel it's time to move on to your next opportunity.

❏ In addition to financial compensation, consider growth potential and contacts when making decisions about your future.

❏ You may need to pivot when necessary, so that you can be in the right position to set your life on its best path.

LESSON 4:

AUTHENTICITY

Authenticity is what the "A" in IMPACT represents. Being authentic means that you must be who you truly are at all times. You really can't be anyone else but yourself, anyway. Being truly who you are and trusting yourself will always pay off. When you are authentic, you will never regret the choices you make in your personal and professional life. To put it simply: you do you.

CONVICTION IS THE ONLY COMPASS

When I joined the promotions team at Arista Records, it was as a local representative in Washington, D.C. Getting the job was not an easy road. Arista had already pegged someone for the position but was holding gratuitous interviews. By the time I had applied, Arista was no longer interviewing applicants and was ready to announce its selected candidate. Not only would I have to sell myself, I would also have to give their executives a reason to believe that re-opening the interview process would be worth their time *and* change their minds about their current candidate of choice.

It took some time, but once they confirmed my interview, I took the train from New York to Washington, D.C. I called the office and got the names of the two interviewers. Then I did my research until I knew the company's background, market trends, financials, and strategy. A black suit, a pair of shined wingtips, and a briefcase comprised my attire. I wanted to represent myself as a professional.

The interviewers rattled off question after question, but I was prepared and gave impressive answers to everything they threw at me. At the end of the interview, I made it clear that I wanted the job. Being direct in my asking happened naturally from my sales background. Immediately after the interview, I discovered where they were staying, and slid handwritten thank-you notes under their respective hotel room doors. The day after the interview, I overnighted thank-you cards to their offices in New York, waiting to be received when the interviewers returned on Monday.

Since they already had a front-runner candidate, the odds were stacked against me. However, I knew that it wasn't over until it was over and that my interview left the door wide open. If I had a chance, albeit a small one, I was going to shoot my shot. In the end, I realized the power of persuasion and the victory of a well-executed plan, namely, quiet confidence and well-thought-out preparation.

To get the interview at Arista, I did not change to fit a mold. Instead, I did things that were authentic to who I was and continue to be. For instance, I naturally enjoy old-fashioned gestures like handwritten thank-you notes and follow-up messages. Being consistent in who I am and what I believe has always benefited my life and career. Also, the move to Arista further supported my certainty.

I worked as the Regional Director in D.C. over the next year and a half. At that time, Arista was the Rolls Royce of record companies. Its roster of superstar artists included Whitney Houston, Aretha Franklin and powerhouse labels, LaFace Records and Bad Boy Records, to name a few. Being a member of the Arista family exposed me to effective artist development and gave me a true education in the business side of the industry. In addition, having other companies as comparisons showed me how much Arista had it together. While other labels were more like creative entities than businesses, Arista was able to strike the perfect balance. Clearly, it operated as a well-oiled, organized, and efficient machine.

Listen to Your Gut

When I was in high school, my dad was strict. He had created specific rules for me to provide structure in my life. One night, six friends came to our house in a van. They were heading to a party out of town and wanted me to join.

When the door opened, we all nodded and asked, "What's up?" Then I looked over and saw a familiar face of a kid who was always getting into something. He was known for being reckless and ruthless, and I knew he was trouble. He had a reputation for being a loose cannon and seeing him gave me pause.

My intuition, or sixth sense, told me to stay behind. This time, I listened. I told the guys to go ahead without me. They started egging me on to get into the van. As I stood my ground, they called me all kinds of epithets. Finally, I told them, "*I'm good*," and walked back into my house. They closed the door and headed to the party. The next morning, it was reported that one of the guys had killed someone. According to reports, the victim's girlfriend held him as he bled to death in her arms.

That night still haunts me. I wonder what would have happened if I had jumped into the van. Would I have been able to stop what happened, or would my life have taken a bad turn just as theirs did? Moments like that night taught me the value of standing my ground and the power of conviction. Some people will apply themselves in life and business, and some simply desire to walk the easy path. If the latter prevails, you will sow those seeds along with them. Remember that you must define your own character and be led by your spirituality and convictions.

Someone is Always Watching

When I think of my time at Arista, I remember the idea of *getting it done.* As a promotion rep, it was my responsibility to convince radio stations to play music from the artists we promoted. Once again, the equity of the company got me behind closed doors and followed with conversations that my name alone could not guarantee.

My biggest success story took place during the time I worked with R&B artist, Monica. She was an Atlanta-based singer, but no one was playing her music anywhere in the country, including her hometown of

Atlanta, which was a tough market to penetrate. Atlanta continues to be in the top tier of urban billing and overall music markets in the United States. The goal was to get Monica's song *Don't Take It Personal (Just One of Dem Days)*, played on the radio. I wanted to be the first Arista rep in the country to achieve that goal. Members of our entire promotional team received their CDs to distribute to their respective radio stations at the same time, and I was the newest and the youngest member of the team. Upon receipt of my shipment, I drove from Washington, D.C. to WCDX in Richmond, Virginia, and pitched the song to the program director. I persuaded him to take a chance and to put it on the air immediately.

It was the first time Monica's song was played at any radio station, and the response was overwhelming. The music quality, coupled with Monica's talent, made her record a hit. The rest is history. That win changed my life for the better. It was a defining moment and made me realize that I wanted to be the best radio promotions person in the country.

After a year and a half at Arista, I was offered an opportunity at MCA as the National Director of Album Promotions. Subsequently, Arista matched the offer by extending my current position to the role of super-regional. The assigned market would now include the Northeast and Mid-Atlantic territories.

My decision was between an expanding territory at Arista, based in Washington, D.C., or taking a larger role (with national responsibilities) at MCA in New York. The pay was the same, but the growth potential was drastically different. I wanted to get back to New York and expand my skills, so I left Arista and went to MCA.

My first year and a half was mostly spent on the road, developing solid relationships with every program director across the country. I was hired by the president of Urban Music, but within the first couple of years of my joining the company, there was a major shakeup, which resulted in both the president and his number two exiting the company. Once the dust settled, I was left as the interim head of urban promotions, a position I had never held before.

Although I was inexperienced in the role, I showed up every day committed to performing at my highest level. I quickly filled the gaps of anything I did not know by studying and asking questions, and I began to thrive. You know the adage, "You never know who is watching you?" Well, that was certainly true here. The Head of Pop Promotions became the Executive Vice President (EVP) of Promotions and chose me as her Senior Vice President (SVP) of Promotions. The general manager was unsure of his decision to promote me; he did not want to risk having someone so green fill that role. However, the EVP convinced him that I was the right choice. I believe that it was due to how I handled myself during the transition. Instead of complaining about what I didn't know, I focused on what I did know and educated myself while staying dedicated and showing my value.

AUTHENTICITY HIT LIST

- ❏ Stay true to yourself and trust that your instincts will pay off, even if the matter is not immediately clear.
- ❏ Never change who you are to fit into someone else's mold.
- ❏ You are your product. Make sure that you know how to sell yourself.
- ❏ First impressions are lasting. Always show up looking the part.
- ❏ If there is a chance that shooting your shot will result in achieving your goal, _never_ hesitate. Take your shot.
- ❏ Be AUTHENTIC so that you never regret the choices of the person staring back at you in the mirror.
- ❏ Do your research!

CONNECTIONS

The connections you have with others can make positive or negative changes in your life. Connections also represent the "C" in the IMPACT acronym. It's important to be connected to those people and things that are aligned with what you want in life. If you find that they don't, then it might be time to make a change. This chapter explains the importance of connections and how I manage my connections to those around me.

EVERYONE HAS A ROLE & A RULE

As human beings, it's natural for us to crave compan-
ionship and relationships with other people. That's why
people date, attend events, and spend hours scrolling
through social media. We want to connect with others.
However, forging relationships and creating *genuine*
connections is a process which takes time to develop. It
is not something we can produce with the snap of our
fingers or with a right swipe on the screen. I've learned
that taking time to build a relationship in the beginning and not force-fitting a connection in the middle
or the end always produces a stronger bond, whether
personal or professional. However, we have grown
accustomed to quick solutions and fast results, so the
problem tends to be in the degree of our patience or
lack thereof.

A friend once confided in me about problems she
was having in her romantic relationships. It seemed
they would always fail even though she was giving her
all. I listened to her words intently and knew that she
was speaking from a place of vulnerability and concern. She was at a loss for why things were not going
her way in matters of love since she really wanted to get
married and start a family.

After she finished giving me some background on
her current relationship, I told her the truth. She was
starting out investing one hundred percent in the rela-

tionship and expecting her partner to do the same. She was open and honest, and while these are admirable traits, not everyone deserves all of you from the start. I asked her to tell me where the relationship could go if it's already at the highest point on day one. The only way to go forward is to maintain at one hundred percent, which is virtually impossible. In trying to bring the best version of herself into a romantic relationship, she was sacrificing her goal. Instead, I suggested that she increase her level of commitment, based on benchmarks. Build on commonalities first, and then allow the relationship to be tested and tried through life's natural processes.

That guidance extends beyond romantic relationships and is applicable to all relationships, even business. Being under pressure or outside of the purview of the public eye reveals more about a person's value system and their personal convictions than a ten-minute conversation at a social event or on social media. Eventually, time will expose the truth about them. That's why I recommend taking sufficient time to learn the "what" and "how" of a person: what they stand for, what they believe in, what they really mean when they speak, how they live, how they interact with others, how they manage their family, finances, and emotions, and how they respond to the spectrum of pressure—from stress to success.

Theoretically, I believe that you should *mentally* put people in different rooms of a house to remind yourself of the closeness of their relationship to you, therefore enabling you to manage your expectations and disappointments. While some people in my acquaintance make it only as far as the porch, others are those with whom I break bread with in the kitchen. It's all about learning the levels, and yes, there are levels to relationships. I considered that concept because it made sense. People to whom I say little more than, "Hello," will make it to my mental porch. There, we can chat about the weather or sports, always with the door closed behind me and a mounting sense of urgency for the conversation's end.

Other people will be invited inside the proverbial house and offered a seat in the living room, where we can have a cup of coffee or a glass of wine and share stories about our kids and memories from recent family vacations. Then, there are the people who make it to the kitchen. This is a room that speaks of love, nourishment, strength, and togetherness. Not everyone will make it to the kitchen because not everyone merits a seat at my table. With those people, I eat, pray, debate, laugh, cry, and reminisce. We discuss our deepest fears and frustrations without any thought of time. I also have higher expectations and attachments to the people sitting at my kitchen table, as opposed to those standing on my doorstep.

Even the house analogy confirms that you cannot connect one hundred percent with everyone you meet unless you are a machine. For some people, you may reveal only a small amount, because even though you may trust them, you are unwilling to share with them your innermost thoughts and feelings. You cannot talk to them about your finances, religion, or family. Others may have earned the right to receive more of your openness and transparency. However, no one is entitled to the whole of you (except God), so never feel pressured to expose all of yourself to someone who has earned only a portion.

It took a few situations for me to determine how much of myself to give to a mentoring relationship. I needed to assess how much to share, when to share, and with whom to share it with. Furthermore, not every business relationship is a mentorship. In fact, most are not.

In mentoring, the goal is to give without the expectation of receiving anything in return, except for the benefit of your mentee's excelling and putting your guidance to effective use. You invest in someone else so that they can be better, but mentoring is not expected to be reciprocal.

Most of us want mutual value and to benefit from the relationships in our lives, which is a normal expectation. Sometimes, the value comes years later and is unexpected. Other times, it is immediate and more urgent. Regardless, relationships are about giving, not getting. Being open with people starts with trusting that they understand how not only to reap benefits from their connection with you, but also how to sow the benefits into your life as well.

Early in my career, I learned the value of allowing people to earn the expectations I placed on them, and not just assigning them by default. It began with my knowing that money is not my only resource. It's not even my most valuable resource. Time and insight are consistent currencies that can be put to profound use. They have allowed me to connect with people when money kept us at a superficial arm's length. When we establish trust and true connection with people, we earn more of their time and insight. These precious gifts lead to an exchange of value.

In life, we should know a person's *value contribution*. In other words, we should know how the person benefits or adds value to our life, and vice versa. How do your significant other, friends, or acquaintances add to your enrichment, and how do you add to theirs? Where do you both stand with your feelings, intentions, and expectations? Why do you want them to know you, and what is the benefit of knowing them? Why is the relationship even necessary?

Often, we fall into friendships and romantic relationships without taking the time to understand ourselves and our own needs. That was one of the lessons I learned early in my life. Know yourself, your value, and your needs before committing to "I do," or even, "I might."

These are only a few of the pivotal questions to consider in matters of love and life. Time is our most valuable asset, so why throw it away by giving it to undeserving people and situations? Why behave as though we have an endless supply of time? In relationships, connections and conversations that fail to add real value or benefit waste your time on things that have no intended destination. It's the equivalent of joyriding in a car with a leaky gas tank.

I am noticeably clear about where people stand in my life and the value, they bring to it. Lead with caution, listen and watch. Everyone cannot automatically qualify as a "friend." Understand the meaning behind the relationship first, and then allow space and room for it to grow and develop organically.

Choose the people who will play a significant role in your life and have good reasons for allowing them to take up space in your heart, your mind, and on your calendar.

Don't Grade on a Curve
Long before I developed the method of mentally placing people in different rooms of a house, I created a

personal categorization for relationships. It follows a simple grading format, like what we learned in school: *A*, *B*, *C*, and *D*.

The A's. My parents are representative of my A's. They are key people whose IMPACT extends beyond a title, role, time frame, or even physical presence. My mother, an integral figure in my life, has given me every necessary tool by which to live a whole and healthy life. From faith to forgiveness, she exemplifies greatness. Even her love for her children would not override her commitment to God. Seeing her exercise good judgment, consistency, and moral character through good and bad times has been an inspiration and an aspiration. Other A's include mentors, confidantes, spouses, and others in your innermost circle who are not blood relatives. They comprise the foundation for how you frame and navigate all other relationships.

The B's. Although we are born into families with no choice in how things unfold, we can and do pick our friends. Identifying and selecting great friends will benefit you over a lifetime. The B's are your network of friends where there is a mutual desire to develop the relationship and help one another advance. The connection is guided by traits of trust, encouragement, support, and growth. B's inspire each other and want only the best for one another. B relationships evolve over time and require nurturing and transparency. I have developed amazing B relationships in both my personal and professional life. These individuals do not always tell you what you want to hear, but they will be honest and show love, care, and concern for your well-being.

When I was Senior Vice president at MCA, I relocated to Los Angeles. A long-time friend wanted to sell her apartment because she was planning to buy another one. She is smart, savvy, and has a giving spirit. She called me with what she felt was a sweetheart deal for her apartment—a deal that I wouldn't be able to refuse. We talked through the details, and I agreed. She sold it to me for $65,000, which was below market value. When I left Los Angeles a few years later, I sold it for nearly $300,000.

I trusted my friend and knew that she cared about my future. What is more, she was clear that the apartment would appreciate, and she would rather that I receive the financial benefit than someone else (especially given my newfound interest in real estate investing). Sometimes, a B will accept the lesser benefit for themselves if they know it will benefit you. I now own over one hundred units in real estate, and a big part of having this asset is due to my friend's early interest in my success. She is the epitome of the B group.

The C's. The C's are casual, transactional relationships who are mutually beneficial. There is limited transparency and depth, and zero obligations. The names and numbers of C's should be kept in your proverbial back pocket, with the understanding that a connection between the two of you will probably pay off some time in the future. C's tend to have expertise, ability, and access. They can be peers, entrepreneurs, influencers, old friends, and people for whom you have mutual respect. C's are movers and shakers.

Sometimes a C's value is less obvious or immediate, but it will eventually supply either a direct or indirect benefit. My relationship with C's has evolved over the years. As I try to keep my finger on the pulse of the marketplace and within social and cultural conversations, I rely on C's for insight. A quick phone call with a C connection can yield massive amounts of information and opportunity.

With C's, everything is not about reaching new heights, or even about helping you thrive. Although some family members can fall into this category, Cs should not be considered lifelong investments. Sometimes a C can elevate to a B, but significant transformation must occur before that happens.

The D's. It took years of implementation, but now I live a life without D's. In my world, they are the equivalent of an F. To have a "D" in school is to be on the cusp of failure, and who wants a relationship that is considered a failure? Neither person benefits, nor does the relationship produce anything of substance or value. D relationships are born from one of two beginnings: either they have fallen out of the B or C group, or their connection was created during a time out of which you have outgrown. Usually, it is the latter. D's add no value and usually cause more detriment than benefit. Yet some people keep these individuals around for no reason other than feeling obligated to do so. No matter how much you love and care about a D, you cannot expect them to be an A, a B, or a C.

Overall, identifying the relevance and role someone plays in your life is paramount. While we all want to constantly hear echoes of our greatness and perfection, it is better to be introspective and self-aware. Forge friendships and relationships with people who will enable you to grow into the best version of yourself. These are the people who directly or indirectly help you achieve your goals and advance your knowledge.

Success Over Ego

After I had worked several years in California, working at MCA, the urge to move returned. My time there had plateaued, and I had a strong desire to get back to the grit and grind of New York City. My mind was set. At that point, I was contacted by the president of Def Jam Records. It was a great opportunity, considering the strength of the company. It was in New York City, and I would continue to learn and grow there. The only downside was the accompanying six-figure pay cut I would have to accept. I was intrigued because Def Jam allowed in very few outsiders, and I wanted to learn the inner workings of arguably, the greatest hip hop label in the world. So, I rolled the dice, took the pay cut, and bet on the future. It was one of the best professional decisions that I have ever made. It opened doors for the next fifteen years that have paid off thirty times over.

Leadership is a Verb

Def Jam was in a transitional state when I arrived, retooling the executive staff and artist roster. Once the new pieces of the puzzle were in place, we were ready to dominate. We knew that the goal was attainable, but it would take a lot of teamwork and a commitment to excellence. Under the new regime, our team released hit projects from Mariah Carey and Kanye West and signed heavy hitters such as Rihanna, Ne-Yo, Justin Bieber, Rick Ross, DJ Khaled, and Young Jeezy. Having these heavy hitters at bat helped to put the label back on the map as the music industry's leading cultural destination.

After working there for nine years as the Senior Vice President of promotions, I began to look at the bigger organizational picture. Then, without warning, our chairman left the company. He and I had developed an incredible dynamic and synergy as I worked with him to rebuild the organization and make it a success. However, I felt compelled to make my exit as well. More importantly, my real estate portfolio was developing nicely, so I was in a position in which I didn't have to stick around and settle for having less than full support.

During my time at Def Jam, we accomplished a great deal: we had an all-star team, an amazing artist roster, and industry respect. Despite all of this, it was time to move on. Although I exited without a backup plan or another job already lined up, I was both comfortable and confident in my purpose. It was time to rise to the occasion and climb a new mountain... "Mount Epic."

When I first joined Epic Records, it was reminiscent of the challenges we had during my early days at Def Jam. The chairman brought me on as the SVP of promotions. I continued to demonstrate value and was later named EVP of Epic. Although the titles were similar, with only a difference of one letter, my responsibilities expanded greatly. I gained access and visibility to the "back office" of the business, including input in the creation of budgets for finance, marketing, and branding. This step was my first time sitting in meetings where my decisions had global implications, and I felt the IMPACT of my influence.

The EVP role also meant additional capacity to mentor staff members throughout the entire company. I became the face of leadership for the team, and our collective goal was to become number one in the industry. We knew it would take time and commitment, but we were patient and prepared. We signed exceptional talent such as Future, Travis Scott, DJ Khaled, 21 Savage, and more.

After I had spent seven years rebuilding Epic Records, we became the number-one hip hop and urban label. Finally, incredible opportunities came from our hard work, sacrifices, and unwavering focus. For me, helping to build an industry-leading label created my next big career move: being named President of Roc Nation Records.

Being in Tune

When I first got into the music business, I noticed the dearth of Black men with salt and pepper hair. At most companies, you'll see white men who have aged as they have risen through the ranks, and they have gray hairs to prove it. On the other hand, older men of color are exceedingly rare, especially in the entertainment business.

My entrance into the industry was by chance and not because of my ability to play an instrument, read music, sing, or compose a song. Initially, I saw the music business as a unique chance to sell a non-traditional product, not just a way to get a paycheck. Have you ever known that you were supposed to be in a certain place at a certain time doing exactly what you are doing? That is how I've felt throughout my career. I am supposed to be here consuming, living, and experiencing this industry and fully representing the artists as well as the art.

Over the years, I have had a front row seat to music and its impact and influence. Music can be used for healing, falling in love, changing mindsets, and strengthening communities. We don't simply hear music, we feel it. Without warning, beats and lyrics vibrate through us, causing us to think, cry, and reflect. From gospel to trap and everything in between, we express our greatest joys and deepest hurts through music. Whether we know it or not, our lives have their own soundtracks, and we can pinpoint specific situations based on album releases or songs playing in the background. In fact, music can move us toward our betterment or our detriment.

The artists I've worked with are poets and instruments of change. Our work is a living element of history because it motivates, activates, and shifts thinking around the globe. Music is a gift, and my good fortune of being able to help share that gift with the world is not lost on me. Music has defined the lens through which I gaze at the world, and it has shaped my life for the better. When I was a kid stacking watermelons and delivering newspapers, I didn't know how music's impact would be intertwined with my life. Even though I didn't envision it from the beginning, at some point during my internship with Motown, I made music my Plan A. I worked, learned, and grew across seven different record labels.

Then, when I started accumulating assets and understanding the true value of time and money, I established a second Plan A: real estate. I removed the possibility of a Plan B because it implies inferiority. Plan B is about settling or accepting something less than what you want. It means constantly knowing I'm doing something, not because I chose to, but because I had no choice. Music and real estate happened because certain people in my life saw something in me and chose to nurture it. They invested in me and allowed me to live a life where I have the freedom to make a choice and a change. For that, I am forever grateful.

CONNECTIONS HIT LIST

❏ Who and what you are connected to will determine not only your next step, but your *best* step.

❏ The people around you can change the trajectory of your life through their words, energy, and actions.

❏ Evaluate those around you. If they are not aligned with what you want and need for your life, make a choice, and make a change.

❏ Take your time to build relationships instead of forcing connections.

❏ Know the "what [to] do's" and "how [to] do's" of those with whom you interact.

❏ Don't feel pressured to expose all of yourself to someone who has not earned that level of openness and vulnerability.

LESSON 6:

TEAMWORK

T he last letter, "T," in IMPACT represents "Team-work." No one can do everything all by themselves. We need other people on our team to assist and provide the necessary skills, knowledge, or experience. An effective team is made up of people who treat each other with respect and trust. They value each other. It applies to everyone on the team, from the CEO to the newly hired intern. With a talented team of people behind you, any-thing is possible.

THAT WHICH DEFINES US

People often want to know how to become a great executive. They yearn for the magic bullet that will effortlessly accelerate their climb up the corporate ladder. Honestly, there is not a clear or decided path. The climb is different for each person and is based on a combination of what is required, what has been made available to you, and what you bring as added value. There is an aspect of success that is obvious but not always mastered, even by those at the top. I don't mean the functional requirements of hiring and coaching people. I am referring to creating *genuine connections* with members of your team.

Aside from my allegiance to hard work, one thing has remained consistent throughout my career: how much I value the people I work with and am surrounded by each day. In looking back at the relationships I've had at the companies where I've worked, I have seen the impact of knowing something as simple as a person's first name and a few personal details about them. Think about it: would you prefer to hear people call you by a generic term or show that they believe you are important enough to learn your name?

Most people enjoy hearing their names instead of broad greetings and acknowledgements. It makes them feel special, and it shows that you not only think they should know who you are, but you value them enough to know who they are, as well. Connection goes both ways, and as a leader, you must demonstrate a genuine desire to want to know those around you.

As I climbed the corporate ladder, my teams expanded, and it became increasingly more important and more difficult to master the art of learning names. Whenever I start a new position, I ask my assistant to provide a floor plan with everyone's name and office/desk position included. I take the time to learn each person's name, and then I challenge myself by walking the floor and matching faces, voices, personalities, and life stories with each person. Because meetings happen all the time within a company, you never know when your name will be mentioned. So, value everyone within the organization and do so with sincerity and authenticity. It's as simple as learning names and walking the floor.

Companies are ever evolving, which is why, as an aspiring or current leader, you must accept that you won't always have as much visibility. Your focus should be on managing resources beyond the people. You're also required to manage time and information. Even though I started my career in the music industry alongside many others, several did not make it to the top leadership positions. Some did not make it due to differing opinions, inflated egos, or underwhelming performances. Others didn't handle information and timing well: they forgot the importance of managing up and down, with the right information at the right time.

Leaders must be attuned to the needs of the organization. If they aren't, they may put pressure on people who are not prepared, causing unnecessary stress in situations that don't warrant the extra pressure.

As a leader, be prepared to fill in the gaps of your organization at every level. No one person should matter more than the whole. An individual should not threaten or bring down the establishment. Focus on individuals who want to drive the organization forward. Build teams that partner effectively, and that go beyond what's asked to deliver what's needed.

Don't Forget to Keep the Job

Over the years, I have developed a winning formula for breaking new talent. I have taken chances on B-level employees who were dedicated to the team's success and turned down cutthroat A+ employees who were willing to work against the team to only better themselves. As I moved through organizations, I brought with me talented individuals who were overachievers and incredible team players. I've also had to dismiss people once they earned the right to be let go.

Most new assignments come with a steep learning curve, especially for an executive leader. It took me years to solidify my process for building dynamic teams. Over the years, I have hired many people, but not all have finished the race. Often, they would get the job but forget the important task of *keeping* the job .

I've personally hired several hundred people over the years. There is a vast array of people who have forgotten to keep the job. I've had valued employees who suddenly became overly ambitious and forgot where they worked. They became short-sighted and forgot the opportunity they had received and the function of their job. They spent time focusing on promotions or doing work outside the business. They became so involved in these things that they forgot about the job that enabled them to house and feed their families. They forgot about health insurance, and the other material things that are important in securing and holding a position at a major corporation. They tended to just fizzle out quickly.

There are also those who want to land a job only so that they can add it to their resume for the next job. They are there only with the intention of exiting as soon as possible. Ultimately, they don't stay because they can't perform.

I've seen those who have remembered to keep the job, as well. They're the ones who have committed themselves to the program and regimen we require. Those are the people who see the most success.

When I was young, I remember having a conversation with my parents about how to work toward your goals. They told me that I would always have to work harder, be smarter, and dream bigger for my goals to be realized. It would need to be a perfect storm of *dotted I's and crossed T's*. My parents never provided specifics on who I was competing with, but I understood and never questioned their guidance and wisdom to always run my own race.

Those conversations were important because they instilled a heightened awareness of how I needed to operate to achieve success. I could not be average; I had to be exceptional. I had to know more, do more, and convince others of what I knew and what I could do. This mindset led to a strong work ethic and commitment to excellence. It also lowered my tolerance for people who did not subscribe to a winning value system.

In any organization, people need time to adapt to a new system, especially if operations are vastly different from their previous work environment. I believe that managers should realize that each new team member needs time to get acclimated. When employees are assuming a new position, you must give them a chance to learn and grow, while offering support and encouragement. However, after the probationary period, the training wheels come off, and management will now have the tools needed to make a final decision on the performance of new hires. Effective team members who want to keep their jobs or progress to the next level, seek constant feedback during their probationary period. In a perfect world, there would be a three-month, six-month, and twelve-month assessment during the first year of employment. Development and performance benchmarks would be tracked during this timeframe. Unfortunately, most businesses are too busy to keep to those timelines.

Leaders must be willing to make the tough and often unpopular calls. We also have an obligation to make honest and truthful assessments of someone's talents and abilities, even when they are not positive. While building a team means recruiting and training talented individuals, it also means terminating those who do not add value to the organization. That is one of the more difficult tasks of leadership.

Having to terminate someone means knowing that he or she is potentially losing financial support for themselves and their family. This is a serious decision, and I do not minimize the severity of it.

Over time, my feelings for terminating an employee have been replaced by a more realistic view. We undergo a rigorous process of identifying problems, communicating issues, establishing new methods, and providing a timeline for change. If individuals fail to do their part to remedy an issue, they often find themselves up for re-evaluation. It goes back to the grading scale for all relationships. I don't have D's in my personal life, and I don't believe in maintaining a D on my team. Everyone must contribute and add value to the team for it to thrive.

Making Real Opportunities

When I was growing up, my family lived in the attic of a five-family house with limited space and even less insulation. Unlike the other families living on the floors beneath us, our winters were frigid, and our summers were blistering. My mother worked at the post office, and my father worked several jobs.

I thought of my father as the Black MacGyver: he could do and fix anything. Being handy was a plus since he was also the property manager of the house in which we lived. He installed pipes, changed electrical wires, and resolved any other maintenance issues that arose throughout the property.

When the owner decided to move back to Kansas, she "held the paper," or in other words, sold the property directly to my parents. In essence, she became the bank. They gave her $10,000 for a $60,000 house and proceeded to pay the note using funds from the other four apartments within the five-family unit. We lived rent-free, and my parents paid off the debt much faster than if they had taken a more traditional approach, like buying a single-family home.

Our family's health benefits were covered by my mother's job, and it gave my father the freedom and flexibility to do what was needed for the house while still spending time with my sister and me. Seeing the dynamic that was created taught me a simple lesson: freedom comes in owning. I wanted the freedom my father enjoyed, and I decided that I would work toward that goal and create opportunities for myself.

As a novice going into real estate, I did not have business acumen in that area. The real insight and knowledge came much later. The first property I ever purchased was in Englewood, New Jersey. I had the opportunity and enough money to buy three condominium apartments, but I was cautious as it would have killed my reserve. Instead, I purchased one and had two of my friends purchase the remaining units. As a first-time property buyer, I learned the true power of ownership. My seventy-thousand-dollar apartment increased in value to three hundred fifty thousand dollars. Now I had equity that could be leveraged in many other ways to positively impact my life and that of my family.

I became a "brick and mortar" investor and chose investments that allowed me to see my money performing. Every time I received a bonus at work, I bought property, whether it was a condo, a house, an apartment, or a city block in Connecticut. Choosing this path was slower than if I had gone with riskier options, but it has allowed me to comfortably invest and has been beneficial over time. My real estate company now owns over one hundred units throughout New Jersey, New York, Florida, South Carolina, Illinois, and Connecticut.

Over ninety percent of my portfolio is rented to single mothers, the elderly, and working couples. For many of my tenants, we are the first opportunity or the last chance for a new renter, which is a tribute to my parents' journey. Even though many of our units are rented to low-income residents, we know the importance of living in quality. We want our tenants to have a sense of pride in where they live. Our philosophy is to have tenants who have a sense of ownership and responsibility for their property and their community.

One year, I had a unit for rent listed at three thousand dollars per month. The potential tenant offered twenty-seven hundred dollars per month, but I would not budge. Instead, I tried to push her to come up with three hundred dollars. She refused and, in the end, the apartment was vacant for ten months. I lost twenty-seven thousand dollars in rent because of a three hundred dollar "ask" and a lack of flexibility. I wasn't willing to bend and learned that, sometimes, you must be flexible to achieve your goal. That was a valuable lesson learned the hard way.

In another instance, one year we increased the rent by five percent. For one tenant, the additional forty-one dollars was not doable, given her current situation. After paying her rent, she would have to decide between paying for food or household bills. We spoke candidly, and after she paid her utilities, food, and other expenses, she would have only twenty-five dollars left to live on. Upon weighing the options, I chose not only to refrain from raising her monthly rent but to reduce it. Sometimes, prioritizing the human factor over the economic factor is most important. I cannot ask a renter to value what's mine if I am not valuing what matters to them. It works both ways.

Even with the wins and losses over the years, I never forgot the lessons I learned when we lived in that five-family house. My father understood the importance of having your money make money. He diversified and created passive income. He created a life where he did not have to be concerned with someone firing him, because he was his own boss. The lessons he taught me as a young man enabled me to create a path for myself in real estate. I am no longer pressed to accept a job that doesn't fit my overall plan simply to make ends meet. I've been there, done that. Even now, we still own our five-family unit home, and it stands as a daily reminder of my father's example and my childhood goal of freedom.

TEAMWORK HIT LIST

❏ Treat your team with the same respect that you would want to receive, regardless of your position, title, and role.

❏ Allow people to learn, fumble, and succeed before making life-changing decisions for them.

❏ Value everyone within your organization and take the time to learn their names.

❏ To be successful, you must learn to manage time, people, and information.

❏ Having the right team can help you grow and expand in all aspects of your life.

❏ When you get the job, don't forget to keep the job.

❏ Greatness does not come from a single individual. It comes from the power of TEAMWORK!

CONCLUSION

DEATH ON MY DOORSTEP

I kept going in and out of consciousness, experiencing everything in an instant and then nothing at all. When I finally opened my eyes, I glanced around the hospital room, trying to orient myself and understand what had happened. Tension pulled at both arms as straps held me firmly planted to the bed. I tried to move, but not much was within my control. I began to shake as I struggled to breathe, which I later discovered was the result of a twisted breathing tube.

Not much later, the doctor entered to communicate the severity of my injuries. Although wearing a seat belt had saved my life, it also had severed two feet of my small intestine and lacerated my liver, causing me to lose half the blood in my body. Nothing about two feet sounded small and insignificant to me. That's one of those moments I wish I'd listened more attentively in anatomy class. How long is an intestine? If the doctor removed two feet, what would I have left? The doctor kept talking and giving me more details. While he was describing my massive concussion, bulging disc, and L3 and L4 vertebrae fractures, I had only two questions on my mind: where was my family, and did I have a colostomy bag?

Over time, I came to learn what had saved my life. I already knew that God was the primary reason I was still alive, but I also discovered three other unrelated factors. First, we were in a Mercedes-Benz, which was the best car for minimizing impact in head-on collisions. Upon the Benz' impact with the tree, the car's engine collapsed, re-routed, and angled itself under the passenger seat, which prevented it from coming into the car and killing us. Second, we hit the tree perfectly. If we had landed an inch to the left, my life would have ended. Conversely, landing an inch to the right would have ended my friend's life. Third, the car was equipped with *mbrace*—an in-vehicle monitoring and safety service for Mercedes-Benz automobiles. As soon as we hit the tree, the service immediately dispatched the fire and police departments to our location, then called the first number on the preset list of emergency contacts. For my friend, that was his wife. Since we'd left our wives only minutes before and were less than a mile away, she was at first confused, then stunned to get a call notifying her of an accident.

Our wives left the kids at the house and rushed down to the scene and spotted a police officer already standing near the back of the car. The Mercedes' *mbrace* system was important because without it, we would have been at the mercy of a passerby who might have been humane enough to call in the accident. Since it happened in the woods and not someone's yard, it would have taken longer for anyone to notice. Given that I had massive internal bleeding, waiting during those precious minutes would have meant the end of my life.

Most people have no idea about the protocol of what happens behind hospital curtains or in operating rooms. The major decisions are up to the surgeons, and they make them based on their experience, personal beliefs, and the exact situation before them. Therefore, it was up to my doctor to decide whether I would get a blood transfusion or not. Growing up, my mother and I had discussed transfusions, and based on her spiritual beliefs, she was against them. I was raised to believe that the best decision was not going down the path of a transfusion. Little did I know that it was a kismet connection. My doctor was also anti-transfusion and decided to operate on me, with less than half of my blood supply.

The friend with whom I had been in the accident came by to see me on day four. Before he entered the room, I had not given him much thought (mainly because I was focused on my own healing). He was very emotional and apologetic after seeing me for the first time since the accident. I didn't blame him, and I told him as much. We were two people who had endured the same accident, and he just happened to walk away unscathed. My thoughts were less about culpability and more about the obvious lessons meant for me. No one plans for an accident, and regardless of what precipitated my being in the hospital, I was thankful to be alive. My focus was squarely on the big picture and meeting his apology with forgiveness.

Later that day, I woke up to find my parents, my sister, and my paternal aunt standing at the foot of my bed. Later I learned that they all jumped in the car and had taken the thirteen-hour drive up from South Carolina as soon as they heard the news. Due to my mother's Alzheimer condition, my sister, who also lives in South Carolina, stepped up her role in caring for my parents. She's always been the type of person who shows strength in times of crisis; with my accident, her solidity would be no different.

Relationships between siblings can go many ways. They can be loving, competitive, or adversarial, but our relationship was always honest and filled with unconditional love and support. When she hurts, I hurt. If she could not figure something out, I figured it out, and vice versa. My sister is categorically another true *A* in my life.

My wife waited to tell my parents that I was in a terrible accident until after the surgery because she didn't want to worry them while the details were unfolding. Moreover, based on how things looked, there was no guarantee I'd make it. For this reason, there was no need to upset them if there was the potential of having to deliver even worse news later. Either she would have to tell them that they had lost a son, or that they had a seriously injured son. She waited until she knew which call to make.

My father made the initial call to my sister, but when he didn't give her enough details to understand what was happening, she immediately called my wife. Although I later found out that my sister was hysterical and distraught during the phone call, her expression at the hospital was one that exhibited the calmness and strength I had grown to know. She wanted to be strong, not only for my parents, but for me. Since I was in that grave condition (no pun intended), my sister immediately took charge of matters. I knew that I could rely on her to take on the responsibilities I had handled for my parents for quite several years prior.

My wife made the same calculated decision about telling our children. She didn't want them to be overly concerned about my mortality when it wasn't yet decided. Additionally, our son had just started boarding school, and we didn't want him distracted.

I observed my mother's face as she tried to decipher who was in front of her. Keep in mind that for the first few days I had no idea how I looked. No one put a mirror in front of me, and there were none on the walls of my hospital room. My understanding of how I looked was limited to the reactions on the faces of others. Their expressions indicated a truth no medical chart included…I was in a disastrous condition.

While my mother's face was expressionless, my father's face bore the weight of *knowing*. He grasped the severity and understood that he could lose his only son. It was the second time I'd ever witnessed raw emotion from him in my lifetime. His emotions and reactions were my informational mirror.

After my family left, I decided that I no longer wanted visitors. If I was going to rebound from my weakest point, I needed to believe strongly that survival was possible. I needed hope and a heavy reliance of faith surrounding me. Seeing the trembling faces of my friends and family was not going to cut it. Bearing their grief and sadness as well as trying to find my own strength to keep going was already too much and would only delay or derail my healing process. There was no choice but to dig deeper and resolve that life was more important than death; my future was more powerful than the pain I had to overcome.

It was not easy. Every day presented new challenges. At times, when the pain elevated to another level, I considered just letting go and yielding to an easier path. However, I *had* to keep going. I wanted to be with my family and enjoy the blessing of seeing another day. Slowly, I came to believe that there's truth in using one's thoughts to "will" a different outcome; this represents well over half the battle. The only requirement is tolerating the process.

Winners become winners because they hold on when everyone else gives up or gives in. They reach down and find an inner strength to sustain them to the very end. They believe in something higher and bigger than a single moment. I've always thought like a winner, and surviving the crash was reason enough to believe in my own tomorrow.

The next day, the doctor removed the breathing tube. I was still heavily medicated due to the morphine drip. I was only able to stay conscious for ninety minutes at a time, barely able to speak, and wildly incoherent. Consequently, I did the only thing I knew to do. I called the office for an update. When the accident happened, I was an SVP at Epic Records. During that time, I never considered leaving the company or stepping down from my position because I didn't consider myself out of the game. I was just an injured player who needed time to recover, reminiscent of a time when I was injured playing football. It was at this point that I understood how athletes feel when an injury forces them to leave the game. It's humbling to be on top one day and then sitting on the sidelines the next. Players often appear lost, dazed, and confused, which is what happened to me. How do you walk away when you have a passion and desire to still get back out onto the field? How does it feel to be able to participate in your mind, but your body is the main thing stopping you?

Unable to move much, I could turn my head only slightly to either side. Now able to focus on the less critical, I glanced at the purple orchid sitting in the windowsill. It had been sent by a colleague just before all deliveries were rerouted to my home. It sat half-hidden in the shadows, halfway embracing the sunlight. Each day I looked over at that lone flower and saw hope. It embodied life. In my condition, having a floral symbol representative of the very thing I needed to fight for was paramount, especially on days when giving up felt like the better option. That purple orchid represented possibility. It was a simple truth. Better and brighter days were coming.

NO PLACE LIKE HOME

Even though I remained in the hospital for two weeks, I felt ready to leave halfway through the time. My limit fell somewhere between the lack of sleep, monotony with my surroundings, and not wanting to feel as though my life was on pause.

Lying in a hospital bed grew old fast. So did my use of pain medicine. After my surgery and during the two weeks I was there, I found myself anticipating the next dose of whatever medication the nursing staff would give me to put me at ease and mask the pain—but that wasn't like me. Having something possess me or cause me to be reliant on it had never been my thing. The painkillers had to be controlled. For me, it was better than facing an addiction problem on top of everything else I was struggling through. Over the next few days, I focused on facing the actual pain of my injuries, weaning myself off the narcotics by taking the prescribed dose less frequently.

The day on which I headed home was bittersweet. I was excited to leave, but every step from the first one out of the hospital bed, to the last when I finally made it into my own bed, meant more excruciating pain and discomfort. For the entirety of the long ride home, my body responded to every bump and turn. Also, I had to put a pillow between my abdomen and the seatbelt because my midsection was raw and unable to handle the constant pressure.

When we arrived home, it was another slow, tedious process to get from the car, up the steps, and into the house. I needed assistance throughout the entire ordeal. Having no choice but to rely on someone just to take a step was difficult for my ego and my mindset. I'd left home physically fit, and now I was standing beside the car, crouched over, waiting for someone to help me up my own stairs.

In any marriage, you never know what type of bond you've created until your relationship is tested. When you stand before one another, God, and family, and vow forever, it's because in that moment you imagine that the only thing strong enough to separate you is death. When you commit to unconditionally loving the other in sickness and in health, it's typically because the only thing you two know up to that point is health. Sickness has yet to test your boundaries or your circumstances. Before the accident, I was very self-sufficient. Given my condition after the accident, I had to depend on my wife to care for me, and she went above and beyond to help me when I couldn't always help myself. Granted, it never got easier for me to ask for help, so I had to redefine my role; it was a new normal for my entire family.

Even with my thoughts all over the place during those initial weeks back home, my wife was steady. She organized a chart with all my medications and times to make sure that I stayed on schedule and didn't over-medicate. She even made the mistake of giving me a walkie-talkie, so I always knew that someone was on the other end to help with any of my needs. Honestly, the only thing that tested our marriage during that time was my excessive use of the walkie-talkie. Not only is my wife a great mother and partner, but her actions also revealed her to be a great person. If I didn't have her beside me for support, it would have taken me longer to recover and recovery would have been a more difficult road.

For my children, the accident was a unique experience. My oldest daughter came to see me in the hospital. Considering she had to witness my initial pain, I knew she would be strong enough to handle my aftercare.

My son, on the other hand, had no idea about the severity of the car accident until he came home from boarding school, a month after I'd left the hospital. I chose to mention only that I'd been in an accident and not give any details so as not to distract him from his studies. It was his first time living away from home and he needed to focus. Worrying about me would have only added pressure or interference, and I knew he didn't need either, since he was already attending a school for high-performing student athletes. Worrying about a parent dying is too much for a child, and I didn't want to put him through that.

My youngest daughter still lived at home and therefore could not be shielded from the damage or my condition. As I re-learned how to balance my weight when walking, eat food, or do other simple things most of us take for granted, she was there to bear witness, help, and gauge my progress.

After two months of being away from the office on short-term disability, I went back to work. Any day beyond sixty days is considered long-term disability which comes with a twenty to fifty percent pay decrease. Although I knew the extent of my limitations and that no one wanted to rush my healing, I wasn't willing to let pain stand in the way of my returning to work.

During the first couple of months after my return, my boss made the call that allowed me to go at my own pace. I went into the office only two days a week, and the company provided a car service since I couldn't drive. On my first day back, I showed up with my skeletal frame covered by loosely hanging clothing. I was thirty-five pounds lighter and limited in my range of motions. All eyes were on me as I walked through the hallways and into my office. Everyone did their best to create a sense of normalcy and support. I was not a pity project to them. Instead, they knew my strengths and allowed me to rebuild from where I was. My direct team was reliable, solid, honest, and filled with over-achievers. They thrived in my absence and continued to excel after my return. We were a family, and without their having to say it, I knew that they valued me and cared about my well-being.

In hindsight, I should have been out for at least a year due to the trauma alone because once I was able to drive, I still had to use a pillow to separate my healing midsection from the pressure of the seatbelt. I couldn't stand for extended periods, and lingering side effects from the concussion were still affecting me.

Honestly, the accident was a blend of divine inter-vention and God's perfect timing. It was His way of redirecting my path. Before the accident, I committed most of my life to working. We say ideally that we put our families first and the work second, but for most high performers that's untrue. The work takes prece-dence, even when we pretend it doesn't. However, life is about moments, and it is our responsibility to make those moments matter.

Since the accident, I've gotten closer to God, my family, and my core friends. I now treat the time we spend together as a high priority, no longer letting these valued relationships take a backseat to my career. In addition, I scaled back on travel to cultivate stronger bonds with my children. I will always be thankful for these connections.

When my youngest daughter was around five, she graced me every morning by coming into my bedroom, kissing me on the cheek, and telling me she loved me. Now, in a fashion similar to that of my mother, she shows me an unimaginable amount of unconditional love. Even though she is a young lady now, when we walk through the mall, and she still grabs my hand because she says she feels safe having me beside her.

After a couple of months, I was asked to go to the police station and give my statement regarding the accident. While I waited, I stood in the hallway talking to one of the officers. First, we exchanged small talk and then discussed the details of the accident. I told him the story about the officer who held my hand and how important having that human connection was for me. I asked if he knew who was on duty that day. I was determined to find the person who had stood beside me and had held my hand as I lay physically trapped between this world and the next. It was my personal mission to find him and thank him. Imagine my surprise when the officer said, "It was me." He told me he visited the hospital every day and checked with the front desk to find out how I was doing. He is a man of faith and understands the possibility of miracles. Seeing how much he cared about my recovery made me appreciate and respect him even more.

The Dividing Line

Surviving the accident gave me a glimpse into how people perceive me, and the consistent theme was *strength*. As I connected with people, in person or by phone, they'd usually tell me about the moment they learned I had been involved in an accident. They shared what they had been doing, who had told them, and when and how they had felt about it. The recounting by one of my colleague's surprised me. As someone told her the gruesome details of the accident, he ended with, "But he lived." My friend replied, "Of course he survived. Why wouldn't he? He's Super Benny!" In business, she'd come to see me as someone who would never give up on her projects or leave things undone. Her image of me reminded me that we help frame how people see us and what they expect of us. Over time, she came to see me as a strong tower and a survivor because our day-to-day interactions had already demonstrated these qualities.

I could fault the accident for almost taking my life. However, I see it as being a turning point in my life; consider it my pre-accident mindset and my post-accident mindset. Pre-accident, I was stuck in a cycle of constant performance. In the post-accident phase of my life, I am focused on betterment. *On Impact*, the trajectory of my life changed. I now have heightened self-awareness, and I am empowered by every experience that has both taken something from me and left behind things never imagined. I now choose to be surrounded by people who will help me become better: a better father, husband, brother, son, friend, and leader.

Life is filled with lessons which we cannot help but learn along the way. Even when we would prefer to close our eyes and brace ourselves, life requires us to be fully present in each moment.

After I woke up in the hospital, a multitude of thoughts filled my head. I think back on that nearly fatal weekend and consider what could have happened differently. What if I had stayed in South Carolina a day or two longer? What if I had kept my afternoon meetings in the city and skipped the barbecue altogether? I have spent many waking hours pondering the what-ifs, and finally have settled into reality.

The impact of my accident opened my eyes and heart in new ways. Barreling toward a massive oak tree with the certainty that your family will have to bury you in the immediate future changes something in your internal wiring. Loving my family while I'm here is my priority. Likewise, preparing and helping them in every way possible for whatever time I have left is of paramount importance to me. The first instance was unexpected; it exposed how unprepared I felt and how unprepared I would have left my family. Alternatively, now I can be more intentional about my time and my legacy.

Having a solid foundation and grasp of faith has kept me balanced and unwavering along my journey to recovery. When I lived in California, I attended The City of Refuge Church, which helped me understand the depth and breadth of God; the pastor there is an incredible teacher of the Gospel. Worshiping at that church had a transformational effect on everything in my life, including the accident: I do not question God, and I receive each day with gratitude.

I've learned that significant change requires significant effort. It is not a speedy solution, but an intentional decision to be and do better, followed by focused, consistent actions. It's a willingness to look in the mirror, acknowledge obvious flaws, and take deliberate steps to be better. The accident also enlightened me. Encountering impact can happen without warning and without your permission. When it does, it's up to you to learn from it. For me, impact forced a choice, and I chose to change.

As I reflect on the days when my son earned his black belt and I ran the New York City Marathon, the value of those achievements remains within me. Year after year, I strive to push myself to new heights. It is what we all must do as we strive for greatness. I celebrate the IMPACT I have already provided and pray for God's grace to accomplish much more.

Along your journey, barriers will come in many forms including: people who have not been properly categorized, opportunities that end up as derailments, relationships that fail despite your best efforts, promotions that never come, and head-on collisions that are out of your control. Through it all, keep pushing. Keep striving. Remain committed to the IMPACT that you can have in someone's life such as a child, a friend, your spouse, a colleague, or a stranger.

When the accolades and titles are no more, when the bottles of champagne stop flowing, and the parties cease, I will close my eyes and know that I have impacted generations by having been the best version of myself and having done what God purposed me to do—forever living with a constant focus *ON IMPACT*.

ABOUT THE AUTHOR

Decades of dedication and determination propelled Benny Pough to the forefront of the music industry and made him one of today's successful and innovative business leaders. Pough has helped shape the sound and culture of music worldwide, having been instrumental in delivering radio hits for superstar artists such as Jay-Z, Rihanna, Kanye West, Travis Scott, Future and DJ Khaled.

Pough's legacy continues as a master of promotions and marketing, coupled with an unmatched eye and ear for talent. Having made significant contributions to the entertainment industry via executive positions at powerhouse labels from Motown and Def Jam to Epic and Roc Nation, Pough is now blazing his own trail as an entrepreneur.

Recently, he realized the time was right to step out and bet on himself; Pough formed DVERSE Media. This multi-tiered entertainment company will be home to record labels, distribution, publishing, and technology that includes social media.

Prior to DVERSE, Pough was President of Roc Nation Records and served as Executive Vice President of Epic Records, a division of Sony Music Entertainment, where he oversaw day-to-day operations. Pough had previously overseen the label's promotion and marketing strategies as Senior Vice President of Promotions and is credited with leading Epic's urban team to monumental success, including becoming the number-one urban record label of the year in 2017. Preceding that role, Pough was Senior Vice President of Promotion at Universal Music Group's Island Def Jam, where he helped propel Rihanna and Kanye West to superstardom, among many others.

Pough was previously Vice President of Promotion at MCA Records for seven years. He launched his music career as Regional Promotions Manager for Motown Records.

Having worked multiple jobs throughout his life, Pough has always wanted to be an entrepreneur. While working in the music industry, he started investing his bonuses in real estate and eventually created Al J. Britt Enterprises, a real estate management company that has over one hundred units in its portfolio.

After a near-fatal car accident in 2014, Pough had a desire to tell his story. *On Impact: Life, Leadership & Betting On Yourself* is a collection of stories, rich in reflection and vulnerability, that expose the experiences that have shaped his life and career. *On Impact* will be the first book released under Benny Pough, LLC—a division of DVERSE Media.

Pough was the inaugural recipient of the Urban One Honors Record Executive of the Year Award. He was a featured speaker at the ITP Media Group's international conference in Dubai and has plans to grow his speaking profile. Beyond his illustrious music career, Pough's interests include public speaking, mentoring, and real estate investments. He currently resides in Bergen County, New Jersey.

For additional information on Benny Pough or D.Verse Media, visit www.bennypough.com *or follow him on social media @BennyPough.*

A free ebook edition is available with the purchase of this book.

To claim your free ebook edition:

1. Visit MorganJamesBOGO.com
2. Sign your name CLEARLY in the space
3. Complete the form and submit a photo of the entire copyright page
4. You or your friend can download the ebook to your preferred device

A **FREE** ebook edition is available for you or a friend with the purchase of this print book.

CLEARLY SIGN YOUR NAME ABOVE

Instructions to claim your free ebook edition:
1. Visit MorganJamesBOGO.com
2. Sign your name CLEARLY in the space above
3. Complete the form and submit a photo of this entire page
4. You or your friend can download the ebook to your preferred device

Print & Digital Together Forever.

Snap a photo

Free ebook

Read anywhere